TruthQuest™

CALL WAITING

CALL WAITING

HEARING AND ANSWERING GOD'S CALL ON YOUR LIFE

RONALD WILSON

STEVE KEELS, GENERAL EDITOR

Nashville, Tennessee

© 2005 by Ron Wilson
All rights reserved
Printed in Canada

10-digit ISBN: 080543125X
13-digit ISBN: 9780805431254

Published by Broadman & Holman Publishers,
Nashville, Tennessee

Dewey Decimal Classification: 248.83
Subject Headings: CHRISTIAN LIFE \ GOD—WILL
VOCATIONAL GUIDANCE

Unless otherwise noted, Scripture quotations are from the Holman Christian Standard Bible, © 1999, 2000, 2002, 2003 by Holman Bible Publishers, Nashville Tennessee, all rights reserved. Other versions quoted are the NIV, Holy Bible, New International Version, © 1973, 1978, 1984 by International Bible Society; and NLT, the Holy Bible, New Living Translation © 1996 by Tyndale Charitable Trust, used by permission of Tyndale House Publishers.

1 2 3 4 5 6 7 8 9 10 09 08 07 06 05

Contents

Acknowledgments

Clearly I cannot acknowledge all those who have contributed to my life and understanding and, thus, have contributed to this book. Some, however, I must mention. Perhaps one of the finest books to be published on this topic in recent years is *The Call* by scholar/writer Os Guinness. Guinness articulates well the distinction between a primary and secondary call, which I have incorporated here, and I am indebted to him for his clear thinking on the topic. However, as a journalist I chose to take a different approach.

I must confess while I'm writing here that the title *Call Waiting,* which suggests a feature in our modern telephone system, was used by an Inter-Varsity Christian Fellowship leader for a career conference, which he organized for college students in Charlottesville, Virginia. I first heard the title there and lifted it because it seemed so appropriate for this book.

Then, of course, I am deeply indebted to my wife, Mary, who is a faithful counselor, sounding board, and partner in ministry. I admit I didn't always respond promptly to the dinner bell while writing this book, nor, while focused on this topic, did I always remember my responsibilities as a husband and father.

One writer's wife once told some friends at a dinner party that when he gets that dreamy, faraway look, don't worry; he's just writing. And one well-known woman author said that her family knows when she's writing because the quality of her cooking tends to diminish. It goes with the territory.

Finally, I am especially grateful to all those folks whose stories I have told in this book. They not only sat still for several hours while I asked them to rehearse the details of their lives, but they agreed to the exposure that comes to them through the publication of this book.

Introduction

When she was small, Bonnie Straka laid on the floor in her grandfather's study and looked at the pictures in his medical books. Grandma didn't think they were right for a child and tried to discourage her. But Bonnie found them fascinating. She knew that when she grew up, she wanted to be a doctor, like her grandfather, of whom she had heard wonderful stories so often.

Tom Miller had no idea what he'd be. While today he's a research chemist with a Ph.D. and the holder of several patents, he never even expected to go to college when he was young. No one in his family had gone to college, so Tom didn't think too much about a career.

Bill Stuntz expected to go to college, but when he did, he had no idea what he wanted to do. In fact he chose his undergraduate school, William and Mary, not because of the curriculum but because the girls there seemed prettier than those on other campuses he visited. Teaching law never entered his mind at that point.

Jim Nash began to think about being a vet while he was a teenager. In the summer when he visited his grandfather's farm in southern Alabama, he wanted to spend all his time outdoors with the animals.

When she was young, Katherine Leary wanted to be a school teacher. Someplace along the way, she found that too tame for her blood and entered the exciting world of business. Eventually she wound up in Silicon Valley as the CEO of a struggling dot-com company.

Tripp Curtis knew he wanted to go to sea. So he joined the Coast Guard and began to fulfill his boyhood dreams. But God had other plans for him. When he married a woman who had two children, he knew that a life at sea was not appropriate. It appeared that he should begin a business as an arborist, a tree doctor, but he rebelled. Trimming the branches on the neighbors' trees was a far call from sailing the ocean blue. Yet, in God's own time he gave Tripp satisfaction and enjoyment in his job—the job that God had called him to do.

Eventually, all of these men and women found what God wanted them to do and now have a clear sense of being called and equipped by God for what he had in mind for them. They now see themselves as God's children, serving him in what is sometimes called "the marketplace."

This book tells their stories and the stories of other men and women who also have that clear sense of God calling them to a specific place and type of work. Too often today we assume that "calling" applies only to pastors and missionaries and others in church vocations. This view implies that everyone else—butcher, baker, candlestick maker—can do what he or she wants to do. In truth, however, God has a plan for all of us. He has equipped us, and he has a place in his kingdom in which he wants us to serve him.

We also compound this situation by dividing the world into sacred and secular. We act as though pastors, missionaries, and church workers are in sacred work, while doctors, lawyers, and others are in secular vocations. This false dichotomy leads to confusion for many as they seek God's will for their lives. Furthermore we take another false step and create a hierarchy of calling, placing the sacred above the secular. So even if we believe that God has called us to be an architect to design churches, our culture too often views the pastor of that church with a higher calling—to preach the Word of God.

This is a book about calling, about the lifelong quest of the believer, ear cocked toward heaven, to discern divine direction. It assumes not only that God has a plan for his people, but that he desires to reveal it in detail—in his own time, of course—and to grant to each of us the conviction and assurance that we can clearly hear and understand.

However, this is not only another book about finding God's will. It's not a how-to-do-it book with ten steps that will lead you to the right career or college or mate. This book focuses on vocation, on what God has called you to be and do. This book is for young men and women who are facing career choices. But it's also for those believers who slipped into a career path without a lot of thought and now are wondering if this is really where God wants them.

When you get right down to it, this is a book about listening. The discord and harshness of our culture is so overwhelming that it takes a special effort on our part to hear the voice of God. The bright lights of the carousel distract us, and the music drowns out any message God might whisper. It takes a special effort on our part and time set aside especially for the task to hear what God is saying to us and to read the obvious signs he has left for us. This book then is about an attitude toward God and a relationship with him that will yield complete assurance and awareness of the hand of the heavenly Father guiding our lives.

I'm a journalist by trade, so I've chosen to tell stories about people in many corners of the marketplace. These people are where they are because they have listened to God and believe that he has led them there. For some it took many years before they had that assurance. Some, who became believers in midcareer, realized that while they had not followed God before this God had his hand on them all the time. Now, however, these folks get up in the morning with a sense of mission, a sense of calling. This is not just another day in their lives. It is a day in which God has a purpose for them. They go to work with a little skip in their step believing that the people in their path, the tasks they must accomplish, and the challenges they face are ordained for them.

Career choices are difficult. Even without the ability to see even a day ahead, we instinctively know how significant they are. Studies have shown that quite a large number of people in the workplace today find very little satisfaction in their work. Who wants to get stuck in an office from nine to five when it's quite clear (at least at that point) that the person is better equipped for an outside job? Or who wants to spend a lifetime teaching in a classroom when it's clear that he or she would prefer to be in business?

You may have a good idea at this point just where you believe God wants you. Then again, he may have something waiting for you that you could never imagine. Before you finish this book, I'd like you to be certain of four things:

1. He is calling you.
2. He does have a place where he wants you to serve.
3. He will reveal it to you.
4. And he will prepare you for it.

You may read this book on your own, or you may read it as part of a group and talk about it with others. Listening to other people tell their stories and/or voice their questions, fears, doubts, and concerns can be a great help in discerning God's will for you. However you do it, I urge you to take time and work through the questions I've added to each chapter. Don't just slip into a vocation because it's the path of least resistance.

On the other hand, you may have strong gifts and, thus, a strong interest in a particular field, and it is the easiest path for you.

I suspect that if you're a typical reader of this book, you're searching and wondering where and how you'll spend the productive years of your life. Well, enjoy the search. Getting there may be one of the most profitable times of your life. Keep in mind that we weren't all placed here to accomplish outstanding things for God, at least as the world measures them. In fact I'd go so far as to say that God doesn't even need us to accomplish his purposes in this world. No, I believe that he has put us here for his pleasure, and he'll be most pleased if we give him our hearts along with giving back to him the time and gifts and strengths he originally gave us.

Also, enjoy the stories of others who searched and to whom God made his will known and notice how he worked in their lives.

Part 1

The Sacred and the Secular

CHAPTER 1

Down with Dualism

Doug Wallace loves to take a risk. You might say that he knows when to hold 'em and when to fold 'em. He's not a bad poker player and enjoys the game, but that's because he has a gift for managing risk. He has done bungee jumping and scuba diving and for several years owned a motorcycle. Those activities may not qualify him as a big risk taker, but one aspect of risk management is knowing just how far you can go toward the edge, then backing off. His calling, as he sees it, is to apply this gift to the business of making money and to use it to advance the kingdom of God.

Doug was brought up in a working-class family in a cinder-block house in Baltimore. His father worked in the shipyards and Doug found work there in the summer. He went to Case Western University on a full scholarship and discovered his gift there while playing poker. After college he got a job in a bank where he met John, who would become a lifelong friend. Neither one of them had the temperament to work in a bank, so they opened a shop and began managing a portfolio of other people's money, by doing arbitrage on the bond market. They did so well that after five years they closed the operation, and, in response to what they had been learning about Christianity, attended classes for a year at a Christian study center. There, as new believers, they began to build a view of the world that included the purpose of work and of making money.

Eventually they both went to work for a bank, managing the bank's investments. They did well, again, but, feeling restrained with the bank's limitations to make quick decisions—so necessary in the kind of investing they were doing—John left and in time went to work for several investors in Texas. Doug stayed where he was living in Richmond, Virginia, but when the bank was sold, he had the opportunity to move to Atlanta and make more money. After consultation with Joanne, his wife, he decided he was supposed to stay in Richmond.

He toyed with the idea of becoming an investment advisor, but he had tried that before and learned that it took 90 percent marketing skills—not his gift—and 10 percent investing ability. So, still in his forties, he was left with the question, "What am I supposed to do? I have these skills and experience and I enjoy making money for the use of God's kingdom, so what should I do?"

Doug was a member of a young, growing church, and he saw an opportunity to help the pastor, so he signed on as a volunteer to assist the pastor using his administrative and analytical skills. Doug knew that church-related work was not a higher calling than that of nonchurch workers, but he might have been seduced by the modern dualism that says that church-related work is "ministry," unlike so-called "secular work." It turned out to be six months of frustration with little joy or feeling of reward. "I felt no success, joy, competence, or vision for doing it," he recalls. So, a sad but wiser man, he left the church to wait on God to learn what he was supposed to do.

"I wasn't on a quest," he says. "When I was younger I might have given myself thirty days to find my place. I knew the Lord would lead me when he was ready, so I settled in to wait. I had a good friend whom I had been advising on financial matters just as a friend. He had just sold his company and went from saying casually, 'Why don't you manage my money?' to, 'Would you please manage my money?'

"It became clear to me that here was a way to use my skills and serve the Lord. This friend has the ability to make money, and he's a very generous man who can provide a lot of support for the advancement of the Kingdom. My role is to alleviate his concerns about his finances and expand his understanding of biblical stewardship. I've learned that there are others out there with that ability, but it doesn't feel satisfying to them at times. They need to understand that they have a place in God's economy as 'givers.'" Since then Doug has found a few more folks there who have the same understanding of biblical stewardship, and he now has a comfortable practice as a registered financial advisor.

"Most people are afraid of risk," he says, "and I probably fall off the horse on the other side. But that's what I do. I'm not about picking stocks or managing your investment return. I'm about managing your risk. Many people would like to go through life without taking a risk, but we can't. We're forced to manage risk, family or financial."

Doug's philosophy of stewardship has given him peace where others have chewed their fingernails. "After 9/11 when the stock market was closed, Joanne and I went on a two-week camping trip. I had done my best in managing my clients' assets. If God wanted to take it all away, so be it. It's his money. It's not ours to fret over."

The dualism that Doug bumped into when he went to work at the church is, unfortunately, prevalent in our society. It says that life is divided into the sacred and the secular and that the sacred is a higher realm. The pastor or the missionary is "called to ministry," but the banker or the line supervisor or the engineer, this view implies, just has a job. The latter may or may not enjoy what they do, and they can certainly live for God on the job, but they're not called in the same way as those who are engaged in "full-time Christian service."

For Doug, it meant that he had to learn what it meant to minister in the marketplace, which initially was a bank. First that meant doing the best job he knew how as a risk manager. "Next it was a matter of building relationships," he recalls.

Sacred Versus Secular

Unfortunately, in evangelical circles today we use the term *ministry* loosely. We say, "So-and-so is going into the ministry." We talk about "laypeople" as opposed to "ministers." This further confuses a concept that is already misunderstood and reinforces this false dichotomy. We are all called to ministry of one form or another. In his book *Called to the Ministry,* Edmund Clowney writes, "Clearly the member serves best who does heartily what he is given to do as a good steward of the grace committed to him. There are no useless gifts of grace; there is no Christian without a ministry."[1]

Quaker theologian Elton Trueblood put it this way: "The ministry is for all who are called to share in Christ's life, but the pastorate is for those who possess the peculiar gift of being able to help other men and women to practice any ministry to which they have been called."[2]

In her biography of Sam Shoemaker, *I Stand by the Door,* Helen Shoemaker wrote,

> We often behave as if God were interested in religion but not in life—in what goes on in church, but not what goes on in a mill or on a farm or a broker's office. This point of view overlooks something. It forgets that Christianity began, not when religion got carried up farther into the skies, but precisely when it was brought "down to earth." It has often been called the most mate-

> rialistic of all religions, because it is constantly concerned, not only with a God above the skies, but with a God who came to earth and lived here. . . . Jesus coming into the world has forever banished the idea of the incompatibility of material with spiritual things. I say without hesitation: there is nothing more "spiritual" or holy about going to church than about going to the office, if you go to both places to serve and obey God.[3]

Dorothy Sayers is quoted as saying, "In nothing has the church so lost her hold on reality as in her failure to understand and respect the secular vocation. She has allowed work and religion to become separate departments . . . she has forgotten that the secular vocation is sacred."[4] A vocation is sacred because it comes from God, not because it accomplishes a certain amount of good for God. The famous Dutch theologian Abraham Kuyper, who at one time was also the prime minister of the Netherlands, wrote, "There is not one square inch of the entire creation about which Jesus Christ does not cry out, 'This is mine!'"[5]

Unfortunately, many Christians in the marketplace believe that it's not sufficient to serve God by doing the best job they can, by being the best physician or investor or chemist they can possibly be. They insist on seeing their workplace as a fishing pond for Jesus, a place to find souls who need God. Sometimes this takes the form of passing out literature or seeing who they can engage in God-talk at the watercooler. Actually, in so doing, they might be stealing their employer's time, which doesn't please God. We don't have to believe that God put us in a particular place for any other reason than to do the best job we know how and thus glorify him. He doesn't give us a quota of souls we have to witness to, like so many pieces of metal we have to stamp out on a machine. He is pleased if we live as his children on the job.

Ron Hansen, a novelist, has tried to inject themes of faith into his stories and has done a masterful job at it. Yet he wrote, "What is good in itself glorifies God because it reflects God. The artist has his hands full and has done his duty if he attends to his art. He can safely leave evangelizing to the evangelists."[6]

This doesn't preclude attempts to minister to people and to testify to our faith in God if it falls naturally into our work pattern. In this book you'll read the story of Bonnie Straka, a dermatologist who often engages her patients in discussions of matters of faith. Bill Stuntz, who teaches law at Harvard, often speaks to on-campus Christian organizations. Tom Miller, a chemist, does not find much opportunity to discuss his faith, but his coworkers know he is a believer and he glorifies God by being a good chemist and caring for his coworkers. Each one sees himself or herself called to serve God, not as a preacher but as a professional in a particular field.

Serving God in the Secular

Many fine Christians have fallen into the trap of viewing their God-given vocation in the marketplace as secular and, further, placing it on a level slightly lower than that of the church worker. It almost happened to none other than the great abolitionist William Wilberforce. His story demonstrates that a biblical view of calling and work can have a profound effect on the world.

Late eighteenth-century England was known for its intellectual life. It spawned such great thinkers as Alexander Pope, John Locke, John Newton, and Edmund Burke. England was also at that time a thriving society with a growing empire and a command of the seas, and was the setting for the beginning of a revolution in manufacturing and industry. London was the commercial and political center where politicians, literary men, and merchants met at coffeehouses and taverns to exchange gossip and discuss the business of the Empire.

William Wilberforce was born into this society in 1759, the son of a highly respected, well-to-do merchant in Hull, Yorkshire. He was born with weak eyes and a weak physical constitution. He was slight in stature with a long nose but with an amazingly strong voice and an active mind.

When he was eight his father died and his mother, not well at the time, sent him to live with his aunt. There he was exposed to Methodists, or Enthusiasts, as his mother called them. John Newton, the former slave ship captain-turned-preacher and the author of the hymn "Amazing Grace," was among those who befriended young William.

However, the Methodists were feared by the established church and society, so William's mother took him away from his aunt and made sure to "scrub his soul," as someone put it, of all Methodist influence. Thus cleansed, William went off to Cambridge where he spent more time playing cards, singing, hosting dinners for friends, and drinking than he did studying. He loved the company of good friends and was an outstanding conversationalist.

Toward the end of his college days, he became interested in politics and made a run for a seat in Parliament, representing his hometown of Hull. In Parliament he renewed his acquaintance with William Pitt the Younger whom he had known at Cambridge. He rose quickly, his intellectual skills were recognized, and he soon became known as an outstanding orator. When Parliament was not in session he spent considerable time with William Pitt, often at a summer home or traveling with him to France on one occasion.

Then came the big change in the life of William Wilberforce. About to embark on a trip to Europe in the summer of 1784, and wishing to have an enjoyable traveling companion for conversation, he invited his former tutor, Isaac Milner. Unbeknownst to

Wilberforce, Milner, while a man of the world in intellect and interests, was an evangelical.

While in Nice, Wilberforce came across a book entitled *The Rise and Progress of Religion in the Soul.* He asked Milner about it, and Milner recommended that he take it with him and read it. The two men read the book together as they traveled, Milner knowing that it was a reasoned exposition of Christianity. The book had a great impact on Wilberforce, who at this point was a practicing Unitarian. Later in the trip as he discussed the book with Milner, who presented a strong intellectual argument for Christianity, Wilberforce began to see the truth in it.

Intellectually honest to the core, Wilberforce was forced to spend long hours meditating on his discoveries and reading the Scriptures. Conversion came slowly, but soon he began to make changes in his worldly lifestyle, and in spite of the potential political liability, he sought out his old friend John Newton.

To explain his conversion, he also wrote to and met with his other friend, William Pitt, now a leader in Parliament. It was at this point that Wilberforce fell into the trap that many still fall into today. He told his friends that he felt he could best serve God in "sacred" rather than "secular" activities and, thus, he would have to leave politics and, perhaps, take up holy orders. Fortunately, for the world, both Newton and Pitt constrained him and argued that God had placed him where he could do immeasurable service that he could not do otherwise. Thus convinced, he wrote to his mother that it would amount to desertion if he left his post in Parliament, and he told his sons years later that he had devoted the rest of his life to the service of God.

Many years before this great change, Wilberforce had become interested in the question of the slave trade that England carried on. His interest had waned, however, in the face of other pressing issues, but with a new outlook on the world, on October 28, 1787, he wrote in his diary, "God Almighty has set before me two great objects, the suppression of the slave trade and the reformation of manners."[7] John Newton also helped to convince Wilberforce to take up the cause of the slaves. Newton had been the captain of a slave ship before his conversion, and he knew the horrors of the practice.

But the slave trade was woven deeply into the financial fabric of eighteenth-century England, and, fueled by greed, it would prove a stubborn foe. Slave ships left England loaded with cheap manufactured goods and arrived in West Africa where the goods were exchanged for slaves. The slaves were taken to the West Indies where they were exchanged for sugar, which was brought back to England for an enormous profit.

The story of Wilberforce's fight against the practice is long and takes many twists. That same year, William Pitt, now the prime minister, persuaded Wilberforce to take the leadership in bringing the matter to Parliament. Wilberforce was not in good health and his efforts brought him near death. He began talking about retiring from public life, but once again Newton persuaded him otherwise. This time John Wesley added his voice, writing to Wilberforce in 1791, "Unless God has raised you up for the very thing, you will be worn out by the opposition of men and devils; but if God be for you, who can be against you?"[8]

Wilberforce continued to lead the charge, and twenty years later, after fierce opposition and continual struggle, on February 3, 1807, the House of Commons voted to abolish the slave trade by the overwhelming majority of 283 to 16.

Wilberforce now turned his attention to the other great object God had set before him—the reformation of the morals and manners of eighteenth-century England. The struggle took the form of many projects to suppress vice, help the poor, provide education, and encourage religion. He gave liberally from his own fortune to help many individuals and societies and saw hundreds of voluntary societies spring up for the betterment of England.

Meanwhile, although the slave trade had been abolished, slavery itself was still legal and Wilberforce refused to rest as long as it was practiced. His strength, however, was giving out when, on July 26, 1883, the House of Commons voted to emancipate all the slaves. Wilberforce died three days later.

For us in this book, the point of Wilberforce's life is clear: had he removed himself from public life, believing that he could serve God better in a church vocation, the world would have been so much poorer for it. By the grace of God, he rejected this false view and continued to serve God in a so-called "secular" place. Who can measure the effect that decision had upon the world? Even his contemporaries recognized the value of what he had done and honored him by burying him in Westminster Abbey. The nation mourned his passing.

To Ask Yourself and Others

1. Think of several Christians you know who work in what we call "the marketplace." How are they serving God in that place?
2. Can you think of occupations in which you can see no possibility of serving God?
3. If you know of an occupation that interests you for the future, ask yourself how you might serve God in that work.

CHAPTER 2

Work, Work, Work

When I was in graduate school, I worked at night in a General Electric television manufacturing plant. My job was to take the television sets as they came down the line on the belt and to turn them around so that the next man in line could put some screws in the back. It wasn't a very challenging job, but I could handle it. I had enough challenge during the day with my courses at the university. However, it did give me some cause to think about the meaning of work, and with the man on the other side of the belt I had some long discussions on what is work. He was convinced that if you liked what you were doing, it wasn't work. Intrinsic in the idea of work for him was that you didn't enjoy what you were doing. And he obviously didn't like what he was doing.

Our situations were entirely different, and I could understand where he was coming from. He had worked at the plant for several years and expected to be there for many years to come. This was his "career path," his way of earning a living. The next step up, he hoped, would be to drive one of the many trucks that moved around inside the plant, shifting boxes and crates. He found very little satisfaction in what he did, and he couldn't imagine anyone enjoying it. He lived for what came after his workday.

On the other hand, this was a temporary job for me, a means of supporting my family and paying tuition while I prepared for the life's work that, I believed, God had chosen for me.

The Significance of Work

Our work has taken on much greater significance in our culture. Someone has pointed out that when we met someone we used to ask, "*How* do you do?" Today the first thing we want to know is, "*What* do you do?" We have become what we do. When someone dies, we observe their passing by noting their work and their accomplishments. Work and worth are closely related in our culture. We draw much of our significance from our work, and we tend to rank people by what they do. A surgeon is higher on the list than a banker, who is higher than a shopkeeper, who is several rungs above the babysitter.

We accept the fact that we have to work without giving it much thought. That's the way the world goes around. It's our economic system. If you don't work, you don't eat. You finish school and go out and get a job. That's our system. It's also biblical, of course. God put Adam in the Garden of Eden to "tend and care for it." The apostle Paul wrote to the Thessalonians, "In fact, when we were with you, this is what we commanded you: 'If anyone isn't willing to work, he should not eat.' For we hear that there are some among you who walk irresponsibly, not working at all, but interfering with the work [of others]. Now we command and exhort such people, by the Lord Jesus Christ, that quietly working, they may eat their own bread" (2 Thess. 3:10–12).

When we begin to think about career and calling and how we'll spend much of our waking hours the rest of our lives, we can't help but consider how we look at the idea of "work."

God's View of Work

So what is work? Did God ordain work and how does he look at it? What should be our attitude toward it? And does God look at the work of a street sweeper differently than he looks at the work of a lawyer? Most of the people I talked to for this book told me that they like hard work. A few said they didn't. One even told me, "I'm really lazy. I don't work hard; I work smart." So he says, anyhow. Yet when he and I went fishing, he sat in the back of the canoe and insisted on doing most of the work, while I did most of the fishing.

My friend at the General Electric plant who thought that all work was something you didn't like would have agreed that work was the result of the curse. (Read the story in Gen. 3:17–19.) But before that, in the Garden of Eden itself, the Scripture says, "The LORD God took the man and placed him in the garden of Eden to work it and watch over it." God made us in his image and he worked—first to create the world around us, then to create us. (Again, see Gen. 1 for the story of creation, which you probably know.) The curse simply turned work, which God had given us as a good thing, into drudgery, straining, and sweating. But when we approach work as worship, something God gave us to glorify him, we redeem it. We restore it to its rightful place in God's kingdom. The Scriptures say, "Whatever you do, do it enthusiastically, as something done for the Lord and not for men" (Col. 3:23).

The poet George Herbert expressed it this way:

Teach me, my God and King
In all things thee to see;
And what I do in anything
To do it as for thee.
A servant with this clause
Makes drudgery divine;

Who sweeps a room, as for thy laws,
Make that and the action fine.

Good Work

C. S. Lewis, the British writer and author of *The Chronicles of Narnia,* made a distinction between "good works" and "good work." When you help Habitat for Humanity build a house or you give twenty dollars a month to support an orphan in Ethiopia or help an old lady across the street—that's "good works."

A good work is when, in days gone past, a cabinet maker or a musician created a work that was superb in every way and would last for centuries. And while it's theoretically possible to do that today, it doesn't happen as often because in the economic world in which we live competition produces something known as planned obsolescence. There is no profit in making the best that you can. The automobile manufacturer doesn't make an automobile that will last thirty years. He makes one that will wear out in a few years so he can sell you another one when that breaks down. Houses and bicycles need repair. So does my washing machine and my computer. The bindings of my paperback books fall apart, and my clothes shrink with washing and wear out. You've often heard older people say, "They don't make things today the way they used to," and they're right. It would slow down the economy if we didn't have to go out and buy new things to replace those that broke.

I have my own definition of good work. It's "doing absolutely the best job I can do in any task assigned to me." And this applies whether I'm making a left-handed widget or cutting peat in a bog in Ireland or doing that mindless task of turning the TV set around on the line at G.E. I must do it all to the glory of God. Keeping in mind, of course, that we are imperfect people in an imperfect world and none of us will create anything that is perfect. Still, I believe God recognizes as good work a job that is done using our gifts and experience in the best way we know how for the sake of doing a good work.

Of course there are also jobs that are destructive physically and morally, and no matter how well we do them, they won't glorify God. The work of a prostitute or an arms smuggler fits in here. And while some will disagree, I see the work of a cigarette manufacturer, as well as the strip miner in the hills of West Virginia, on the same level. So as you make career choices, you have to ask yourself, does this work contribute to society or help destroy it?

Many years ago I wrote a magazine article exposing the sham project of a power company that planned to flood a valley where families had lived for generations so they could build a power plant that really wasn't needed. My article pointed a finger at the power company whose motivation had to be nothing else but making money while they destroyed dozens of family homes and uprooted scores of people. After the article was printed, someone wrote a letter to the editor saying that I shouldn't attack the company because there were believers who worked for it. I'm sure that was true, but their presence didn't excuse the immoral behavior of the company executives. And it put the believers who worked for that company in the place where they should have been asking, "Is my job contributing to the destruction of this valley?" A lineman for the company who spent his days climbing telephone poles and stringing lines was probably not in danger of doing anything destructive. But the Christian man who drove the bulldozer that would tear up the valley and knock down homes had to stop and think twice about what he was doing.

Finding Meaning in Work: Ward's Story

Ward Anderson wasn't afraid to work. In fact he liked it. His problem the summer of 1994 was that he didn't have any work.

He was not, as we say, "gainfully employed." Ward had a master's degree in business administration, had bought out the office furniture division of the company he worked for, and became president of his own company. He soon realized that what he was doing was not a good fit for him, and with black economic clouds on the horizon, he sold the business and became the marketing director of a small private school. Three years into that he realized that was not working either, so he resigned before he had another job. He had saved a little when he sold his business and could live for a little while as he looked around for another business to buy. But that summer he realized that he needed to bring in some cash, so, not being afraid of hard work, he took a job with a landscaping company.

This company had contracts with businesses and individuals to keep their grounds trim and neat and also to shovel the snow from the walks in the winter. Still, Ward wasn't quite ready for it when the boss called him one snowy evening and told him to go next door and shovel the walk. The company had a contract with Ward's neighbor. As he shoveled away, the front door opened and his neighbor's wife stuck her head out and said, "Is that you, Ward?"

"It sure is, Marjorie," he answered. "I'm in transition."

It was a little embarrassing but nothing to compare to what was to come. He was in the downtown office section where the town's prominent attorneys had their offices. Ward knew many of these men, had gone to school with them, played tennis with them, shared meals. Part of the landscape company's contract called for keeping the street clean in front of the offices, so the boss asked him to clean up a certain section. Feeling self-conscious, he put on a pair of sunglasses and pulled a baseball cap down over his eyes and began sweeping up the dozens of cigarette butts that were littered on the sidewalk and in the gutter. He soon had a big pile of them and asked his supervisor what he should do with them. "Go back to the truck and get a broom and a trash can," he was told. Not wanting to run into anyone he knew, Ward decided to kneel down in the gutter, and he started stuffing the cigarette butts into his pockets. It was a moment of truth that he never forgot.

"Before that," he recalls, "I would have looked at a street cleaner and thought, *I'm glad I'm not like that.* But as I stood up that day, I was a different person." The Ward Anderson who had an MBA, had been the president of a company, had graduated from prestigious schools, and whose father was a doctor, was severely humbled. *Never again,* he thought, *will I ever look at people through the filter of my position and accomplishments.* "I knew then that I was no different from the migrant farm worker or the man who flipped burgers at McDonald's or the stable hand or the washerwoman. We were all equal in God's sight. What makes the difference is how we look at what we do."

What is it that gives value to our work? Paul wrote in one of his letters in the New Testament, "Whatever you do, do it enthusiastically, as something done for the Lord and not for men," (Col. 3:23). God declares our work important, whatever it is, as long as it's done to bring glory to him. Martin Luther wrote, "With persons as his hands, God gives his gifts through the earthly vocations, towards man's life on earth: food through farmers, fisherman, and hunters; external peace through princes, judges and orderly powers; knowledge and education through teachers and parents. . . ."

A few years later Ward found meaning in his work using his natural gifts and his training. As he continued to search for a suitable business to buy, he thought about a friend to whom he had sold office furniture years before, and he remembered that this man owned some apartments. Ward owned several houses in his town, from which he earned a small income, and he thought, perhaps, this might be a way of earning a living. So he contacted his friend, Buddy, and they had lunch at Buddy's country club. As the lunch closed, Buddy handed Ward a professionally prepared portfolio that described the apartments and explained why they would make a good investment. Ward quickly noticed the asking price—$6.1 million for the 166-unit complex.

Ward is nothing if not forthright and honest, so he quickly explained to Buddy that he couldn't come near that amount. After some negotiation and a meeting in an attorney's office, Buddy surprised Ward by telling him he'd finance the remainder of the price after Ward had raised what he could. So in a few months Ward and Martha Hayes, his wife, became the proud owners of an apartment complex that they promptly renamed Meriwether Hills, after their daughter.

In a short time, Ward began finding fulfillment in dealing with the tenants. They were, for the most part, blue collar workers including some single mothers and some newly arrived immigrants. He remembers the middle-aged woman with five children from Uruguay who cleaned motel rooms at night. One evening on her way home, she fell asleep and her car hit a concrete abutment. The woman ended up with severe brain damage. Folks in the complex came to help and eventually relatives came from home. Ward cut her rent in half and forgave some back rent that was due. Soon some of the children attended the Vacation Bible School at Ward's church.

Originally Ward had dreams about how he'd use the apartments as a place to minister to people. Ward is a visionary who sees great possibilities in a project and knows how to put feet to his dreams. He thought, for example, that they might have programs such as marriage counseling—things he thought the people needed. But in this case God had a different plan. Several of the pastors from his church, including one young man from Mexico, moved into the apartments, and they are the ones who are reaching out to their neighbors. Among other things they began an after-school program for the children.

Managing 166 apartments, keeping them maintained, and improving the ground is more than a full-time job and Ward, who thoroughly enjoys people, loves it. He is using the skills God has given him, and his verdict on the job God has given him is, "I've learned so much here about loving people."

Embracing God's Work: Tripp's Story

Tripp Curtiss in Marin County, California, was stuck in a job he didn't like and couldn't see any way out. "A man's gotta do what he's gotta do," he grumbled as he picked up his chain saw and went to work trimming trees.

After a stint in the Coast Guard, Tripp had worked as a merchant marine and was working for a tug and barge company on San Francisco Bay when he met Barbara. His job called him out often in the middle of the night when there was an emergency, and it kept him away for days. Barbara had two children when he married her, and they soon had another one on the way. With some persuasion on her part, he realized that his lifestyle was incompatible with having a large family, so he quit it hoping to find another job on the sea, which was his great love.

Nothing turned up, however, so with no money coming in, he turned to his old trade of trimming trees. He began calling friends, people he knew, bidding on jobs while Barbara answered the phone and kept the books. Soon he had more work than he could handle so he hired an assistant. He worked on trees all day, he recalls, and "I dreamed of the sea, especially as summer came on."

At this point Tripp might have taken comfort from the life of John Bunyan. In seventeenth-century England, Bunyan was the son of a poor tinker and had little education. When he married, his wife's dowry consisted of two books. Bunyan read them, and they led him to a life of serving God and preaching the gospel. However, during the reign of Charles II, it was illegal to hold church services unless they conformed to the Church of England. So Bunyan was thrown in jail and prayed daily for release. But God had a purpose for Bunyan to be in jail—while he was there he wrote *Pilgrim's Progress,* which has become the second best-selling book after the Bible.

One day Tripp's assistant called in sick, leaving him with a big job. He already had an aching arm, and on top of that his saw was acting up and it was an especially hot day. He was not a happy camper, and he found himself arguing with God. *"Lord, I just don't understand what you want me to do. Why can't I go back to the water? Am I supposed to be stuck in these trees the rest of my life?"* Suddenly, as he remembers it, God gave him peace, and he knew that this was his calling, taking care of God's creation. What better way, he thought, to support a family, be there for them, and serve the community?

That night when he returned home, he astonished Barbara by throwing his arms around her and saying, "I'm home, honey."

"I can see that," she replied, puzzled now.

"No, I'm really home," he told her and explained what had happened and how he was ready to embrace the gift God had given him. Weeks later a woman at whose house he was working brought him a cup of coffee and told him, "They really ought to call you 'Mr. Trees.'" He and Barbara liked that and began using it as the name of the business. The business continued to grow; Tripp got a license as a contractor and a certified arborist. They hired a bookkeeper, and soon Mr. Trees was in *Inc.* magazine's list of the five hundred fastest-growing businesses in America. Mr. Trees eventually grew to twenty-five employees, and Tripp and Barbara ended up with twelve children, some of whom they have adopted. But most importantly, Tripp, as Mr. Trees, was firmly planted in God's will.

The story of Ezekiel's vision of the Valley of Dry Bones has a beautiful application here. The Lord led the prophet Ezekiel into a valley filled with dry bones. Then as Ezekiel followed the Lord's command and prophesied, the bones connected to one another and took on flesh and finally came to life (Ezek. 37:1–12). The story is about God restoring the nation of Israel, but it can be applied to us as individuals. Tripp and Ward, stuck in jobs of drudgery, asked, "Can these bones live?" And God answered by breathing his Holy Spirit into their lives. Note that it is the Holy Spirit who does it. Both men would be quick to say that if left to themselves nothing would have changed. But their attitude and outlook were radically affected and their lives renewed as the Spirit of God touched them.

Following God and Finding Peace

Both Ward's and Tripp's stories raise a question that many young people ask today: "In this business of choosing a career and charting out a plan for my life, do I have any rights? Or am I supposed to blindly, without question, follow the path it seems that God has laid out for me?" It's not a matter of rights; it's a matter of who is going to be God of your life—you or God. Who knows what's best for your life? You or the one who made you in his image?

To become a believer is to become a follower. Jesus called several of the disciples away from their line of work as fishermen and told them to follow him—which they did, traipsing all over the countryside while Jesus taught and healed. In fact, the words "Follow me" were the first and the last words Jesus spoke to Peter. God called Ward and Tripp to a line of work that neither one would have chosen for themselves.

Dietrich Bonhoeffer, a German pastor whom Adolph Hitler imprisoned then hung, wrote, "When Christ calls a man, he bids him come and die." For most of us that won't mean physical death as it did for Bonhoeffer. It will mean death to self, death to playing God of our own lives, and, instead, listening to what he has for us. The Bible says a lot about dying to self. The apostle Paul wrote in his letter to the Romans, "If we live, we live to the Lord; and if we die, we die to the Lord. Therefore, whether we live or die, we belong to the Lord" (14:8).

Do I make it sound easy? It's not, but it's certainly possible, day by day, as we face decisions. When I was young, I loved the lines of a particular hymn: "Are ye able said the master to be crucified with me? Yea, the sturdy dreamer answered, to the death we follow thee." Even then, in my idealism and naïveté, I knew that those would be empty words if left on my own. But God gives us the grace when we need it, just as he gave it to Ward and Tripp, to die to what they wanted, to their natural selves, and find peace in what God had planned for them.

Strike out on your own to find out what kind of work you want to do in life and you'll fail miserably. A friend of mine just e-mailed me a helpful reminder. "When I feel confident," he wrote, "duty, obedience, goals, and hard work become the fuel for my daily motivation in life. Self-confidence is the drug of choice for many Americans. But then we're feeling weak, needy, fearful, discouraged, and frustrated. It can be a time of rediscovering Jesus himself, seeing him as the Pearl of Great Price, worth selling all to get."

If you have not already had a full-time job, you certainly will in the days to come. Now is the time to sort out how you feel about work. Whether it is what society thinks of as menial—cleaning, shoveling, emptying trash, or flipping hamburgers—or if it's running a *Fortune 500* company or managing a city, God will give you an opportunity in that work to learn more about him and to bring glory to him by doing the best job you know how to do.

To Ask Yourself and Others

1. We said earlier that the Bible says a lot about dying to self. Find several passages in the Scriptures that teach this truth.
2. Reflect on your own attitudes toward work. Do you like hard work? Are you lazy? How does the work you do (part-time, at home, or volunteer in church or in the community) glorify God?
3. Have you ever had to work at a job you didn't like? Why didn't you like it? How did you respond? Did you give it your best effort, or did you try to get out of it as fast as you could?

CHAPTER 3

Who's Calling?

Go to a search engine on the Internet and type in "My Life's Purpose Seminar." You'll find dozens of seminars, books, workshops, audio- and videotapes offering to help you find the answers to life. It appears, to no one's surprise, that we have a deep yearning to find significance in life. Why are we here? What is life all about? Why were we made? How do we find fulfillment and lasting satisfaction? These are the questions that thinking people ask, and the answer to our questions about calling are wrapped up in our purpose in being here in the first place.

Let's make it clear first that we're not talking here simply about career guidance or discovering our gifts. That will come eventually, but God's calling starts back several steps before those questions.

The Primary Calling of God

The first step is to hear God calling us to himself. The Bible makes it clear that God calls us first to himself. One translation puts it this way: "It is God who saved us and chose [called] us to live a holy life. He did this not because we deserved it, but because that was his plan long before the world began—to show his love and kindness to us through Christ Jesus" (2 Tim. 1:9 NLT). God has first called us to himself. He doesn't call anyone to be a pilot or a dancer or a plumber or a soldier before he calls that person to follow him. He puts his name on us—Christian. We are his. He made us and has a purpose for us. "Now this is what the LORD says—the One who created you, Jacob, and the One who formed you, Israel—'Do not fear, for I have redeemed you; I have called you by your name; you are Mine'" (Isa. 43:1).

Scholar and author Os Guinness, in his book *The Call*, defines our primary calling this way: "Calling is the truth that God calls us to himself so decisively that everything we are, everything we do, and everything we have is invested with a special devotion, dynamism and direction lived out as a response to his summons and service."[1]

For many years I had a head knowledge of this because I learned the first question in the catechism, which reads "Q: What is the chief end of man? A: Man's chief end is to glorify God, and to enjoy him forever." That sums up in a phrase why God has called us to himself. For his enjoyment. Paul wrote to the Corinthians, "Therefore, whether you eat or drink, or whatever you do, do everything for God's glory" (1 Cor. 10:31). Paul was talking specifically about eating meat that had been offered to idols, but the principle applies to all of life.

When Isaiah wrote, "I have called you by name; you are Mine," he was writing about the Israelites, but the passage also applies to us today. God has called us. He knows who we are. He not only knows us; he knows more about us than we know ourselves. In fact, when you stop and think about this primary calling of people like you and me by God the Father to himself, it is utterly amazing. David wrote in Psalm 139 (NIV): "O LORD, you have searched me and you know me. You know when I sit and when I rise; you perceive my thoughts from afar. You discern my going out and my lying down; you are familiar with all my ways. Before a word is on my tongue you know it completely, O LORD" (vv. 1–4). The fact is that it is our creator who has called us, and as we contemplate that, we understand David's cry later in the psalm: "Such knowledge is too wonderful for me, too lofty for me to attain" (v. 6).

Still, knowing all this and acting in accordance with it (as though I really believed it) was something else. One time a few years back, perhaps after a spell of frenetic activity of which I'm capable, I discovered that God is more interested in who I am than what I do. I am by makeup goal oriented. I thrive on being busy, having pressing deadlines, having more than I can ever do. So it came as a shock to me to stop and consider that God was not impressed with my busy work, nor did he need it. He can run the world very well without the work of my hands. Instead he wants my heart; he wants my love. That's why he created me, for his purpose.

But we are all stuck with this proclivity to "do" something, seeking satisfaction in our performance and seeking the approval of others. I realized I was no different than most people, only more dedicated or addicted to work than most. So I tried to slow down and focus more on loving God, trusting him, and spending time in his presence. The Scripture tells us that Abraham *believed* God, and it was credited to him for righteousness. It wasn't the good things he did that impressed God. God didn't single him out as the Father of the Jewish nation because he accomplished so much. No, Abraham pleased God because he trusted God. It was Abraham's faith that God noted.

I still have a hard time breaking the performance addiction. As I write this, I'm living in Ireland and working with a mission agency. When my wife and I arrived in Ireland a year ago, our mission agency, like many others today, told us they didn't want us to jump right into our job assignments. They said we needed to take time to adjust to the culture. So we visited the city and some small towns, went to see historic sights, ate at various restaurants, visited shops and churches, and so forth, and talked to as many Irish people as we could corner. One day after about two months of this, I realized that I was depressed and I desperately wanted some assignments, deadlines, and responsibility.

Then one of my mentors from the U.S. got a hold of me and told me, "Ron, you have made work an idol. For years you have received affirmation from your work performance. That's been your reason for being and that has brought you your day-to-day satisfaction. You've done what Jeremiah told the children of Israel they had done: 'For My people have committed a double evil: They have abandoned Me, the fountain of living water and dug cisterns for themselves, cracked cisterns that cannot hold water' (Jer. 2:13). You've been trying to squeeze life and satisfaction out of your work. But now God has you in a place where he has torn that idol away from you, cut it out of your life, and it hurts." I knew immediately that he was right. I had forgotten the old lesson. God doesn't want nor need my work. He didn't call me to himself for that reason. He called me to himself to enjoy fellowship with me and for me to enjoy him. I need that reminder constantly.

So when I come to the truth about God's calling me to him first, and not to a particular task, I have to stop and rearrange my priorities. And that's what you have to do. Before you begin to seek God's secondary calling—where he wants you and what he wants you to do day by day—you have to act on the implications of his primary call to you to be his and in a relationship with him. Os Guinness puts it like this: "Everything we do, and everything we have is invested with a special devotion, dynamism and direction lived out as a response to his summons and service."[2]

This primary call is important. It's a matter of life and death; it's salvation; it's knowing God; it's knowing who made me and why; it has to do with the meaning of life. Why would anyone not want to have the answers to these questions and walk through life knowing the one who made him and live with the assurance of belonging to God?

Beyond that, however, Guinness goes on to give a number of reasons why a sense of calling in our lives day by day is important. Among the reasons he gives is that having a sense of calling is a help to resist the modern-day pressure toward secularization. A sense of God's calling on our lives gives us a glimpse of the transcendent in the world. And a sense of calling can keep me from indulging in envy as I see those around me who have been given talents, gifts, fame, and fortune that I have not been given.

Now, add to Guinness's thesis that everything we do, and everything we have, is invested with a special devotion, dynamism, and direction lived out as a response to his summons and service, "the understanding that he has called us to be part of his family, sons and daughters of the living God, brothers and sisters in Christ."[3] We could fill an entire book writing about the implications of this family relationship. I cite it here because it has such profound implications when we consider our secondary calling. We are not left on our own to figure out what God has planned for us. Not only will he reveal to his children what he wants for them; he has put us in a relationship with brothers and sisters—the visible church—to whom we can turn for help. This is one of the family benefits he has given us—relationships with other believers.

God's Calling Us to Himself: David's Story

I can think of no one I know who has applied this principle regarding calling to his life with more thought and significance than David Turner, a businessman and the owner of Turner Enterprises in Charlottesville, Virginia. David was born in Roanoke, Virginia, the son of the owner of J. M. Turner Construction Co. While still in high school in the summers, David began to learn the construction business from the ground up, as he puts it—digging ditches. David had become an accomplished tennis player in high school, traveling extensively to play in tournaments, and he would have preferred to play all summer. But peer pressure, as he puts it, said that in the summer you got a job. Eventually he became a carpenter's helper, then he drove heavy equipment and slowly learned the business, which he enjoyed. Turner Construction Company built shopping centers, bridges, apartment buildings, sewerage treatment plants, all kinds of projects. David has fond memories of getting up at dawn in the summer and going with his dad on Saturday morning for breakfast. His dad was a fun-loving man with a great sense of humor and a zest for life, and David admired him. They would then spend the morning visiting the company work sites, and it was exhilarating for a teenager.

David's mother was a firm Christian believer, and she made sure that David and his older brother, Jay, heard the gospel and learned the Scriptures. She had a friend named Jane Stuart Smith who had studied with a philosopher/theologian named Francis Schaeffer. Jane, David remembers, was one of the most intriguing characters he had ever met. She soon had David studying the Bible and taking Bible study correspondence courses. He had been blessed with a hunger and an aptitude for learning. "I was a sponge," he recalls. "I soaked it up." At twelve he made a commitment to the Lord that lasted about two years. Then he began to struggle with questions such as why the Lord didn't answer his prayers for his father who was struggling with alcoholism, which exacerbated family problems. Looking back he realized that he was wrestling with the problem of evil. "It seemed to me that God wouldn't do anything about the biggest problem in my life.

"The various aptitude tests I took all told me that my gifts matched my desire to be a general contractor like my dad, so I enrolled in the engineering program at the University of Virginia. The engineering department was a separate part of the school, and I realized that not only was I learning more than I wanted to know about engineering, but being separated from the main part of the university was interfering with my social life. So I transferred and ended up getting a degree in economics."

While he was in college David claims he was a full-fledged hedonist. He met a young woman, Ellen Kennedy, with whom he fell in love and despite some opposition from her family, they were married in the summer before his senior year.

College raised a lot of questions in David's mind that he couldn't answer, and he was still trying to determine what he thought about Christianity. It was time to decide whether he would reject it or embrace it. So, like many young men and women in the sixties, he and his bride took a trip to Europe to find answers. They ended up at L'Abri, a study center in the Swiss Alps run by none other than philosopher/theologian Francis Schaeffer. Partly because of the unusual character of Dr. Schaeffer, the center attracted young people from all over the world who were part of the sixties generation trying to find the answers to life. While at L'Abri, the spiritual lights turned on for Ellen, and David realized that he had squandered his academic years and wanted to make them up. So they decided he would go to seminary.

It's important, however, for the point we're trying to make here, to realize that David did not go to seminary planning to be a pastor, which is why most young men go to seminary. As far as he was concerned, he would someday go back to the construction business. Seminary for him was a way of preparing himself as a Christian for life. In keeping with the definition of calling, which we quoted earlier from Os Guinness, David knew he was called to Christ, and he wanted to explore what that meant, apart from a vocational call. (The irony here is that Os Guinness was then working at L'Abri, and he was the one who directed David to Trinity Seminary.)

To become a believer is to become a servant and a follower. Landscape gardener, lobster fisherman, atomic energy scientist, law school professor—wherever your gifts and interests lead you, that is secondary. Unfortunately most Christians focus more on "how to make a living" than on "how to live." And they focus more on 401K plans and stock options than on the mission of the church. Money, without question, is important. But nothing in the Bible gives us reason to use the size of the monetary reward solely as a means of deciding which vocation to follow. Nor does following Christ and trusting him guarantee physical comforts, much less luxury. We take away the sense of calling when we reduce it to benefits and fame.

For David Turner, deciding what God wanted him to do specifically with his time and talents was secondary to his commitment to know God. In time God directed him back to the construction company. He had considered going on to Aberdeen for a Ph.D. but the company needed him, so for four years after leaving seminary, he worked to consolidate a company that was fragmented and needed pulling together.

During his last year in seminary, David discovered a special gift that he had and enjoyed—teaching. He was given a chance to teach Greek, and while he felt he was in over his head, he had a good time doing it.

In 1978 he was asked to come to Charlottesville, Virginia, to take over a Christian study center that operated on the edge of the University of Virginia campus. He developed a one-year curriculum for people like himself who were not planning on going into church-related vocations but wanted a greater understanding of their faith and more preparation to live out their call to Jesus Christ. He did this for seven years and loved it. With his academic bent, he loved the preparation as well as the interaction with serious learners. But increasingly he felt isolated from nonbelievers. While he was teaching folks how to live in the world as salt and light, he was not living in that world. His work kept him mostly in contact with a small evangelical subculture.

He also admits another tension existed at the time—income. He had been brought up in a different socioeconomic environment than he was then living and wanted to provide for his children the kinds of opportunities he had had. How much this affected his decision he's not sure.

So he began to think about going back into construction. But he also knew that he missed the world of business. Today he says, "I think that calling is part and parcel of what we call providence. We are who we are because of what happened for generations. We don't suddenly appear at any moment without a history or without genetic or environmental influences. Nor does God suddenly begin to work in our lives, preparing us for a vocation, the moment we become believers. That began generations ago. We also grow up with our parents' expectations, and it's hard for us to get away from that."

Of course this kind of wisdom does not spring full bloom to us when we're young. David reflects on those earlier years and says, "In my thirties and forties I had a vocabulary to express a thoughtful Christian position, but I don't think I saw how much my ego was wrapped up in wanting to 'do' something. I think that even the process of discovering what God wants us to do is wrapped up in Christ just as our primary call is a call to Christ. We are called first to a person. Then we draw all of life from him. He prunes us; he cuts away things that are unproductive; we go through seasons that are not as fruitful as we'd like. We live in a culture that is oriented to accomplishment, but one wise teacher told me that God has more to do in me than through me. We don't easily see our ambition, and the Lord graciously uses that ambition at times, but I believe that what he wants first is our complete surrender to him so that he can restore and empower the gifts he has given us."

In 1988 David started his own company doing commercial and industrial development and construction. He enjoys putting deals together as well as pulling together the contributions of many people like real estate agents, funders, architects, accountants, estimators, and construction people. He compares managing the process to that of an orchestra conductor who knows what each instrument can do but can't actually play the instrument. Instead, the conductor brings them all together to produce a pleasing result.

Then David tells one story that illustrates much of his view on calling. He had once explained his view to a friend who worked as a distributor of retail groceries. His friend looked at him, scratched his head, and asked, "Will you tell me how restocking the fruit coop has anything to do with the kingdom of God?" David didn't have a ready answer. Several years later his friend died, and at his funeral David heard testimony after testimony from friends who had been touched by this man as he worked alongside them. For David, that said more about Christ's primary call to himself than all the theories in the world.

To Ask Yourself and Others

1. As it relates to your life, explain to a friend this idea of a two-step process of calling—first to Christ, then to a specific vocation.
2. How does your relationship to Christ impact you and how do you think it might affect your search for a specific vocational calling?
3. Does the desire for a comfortable life or for fame or power or simply for approval affect how you think about your calling?

CHAPTER 4

It All Began in the Bible

The Bible is filled with stories in which God calls men to himself as well as for specific acts of service. God told Abram (whose name he changed later to Abraham), who was a very old man at the time, to pick up his family and move to a land that he would show him. He spoke to Moses out in the desert from the middle of a burning bush. (That would get my attention too.) In an audible voice, God called Samuel in the middle of the night. Then he called Esther to be queen at a special time in which her people needed help, and he did it in a roundabout manner. He called David to be king by pointing out the shepherd boy to Samuel the prophet.

In the New Testament we have stories of Jesus approaching Simon Peter and Andrew and James and John as they were preparing to go fishing and telling them to follow him. Then, in a dramatic confrontation, he forced Saul (whose name became Paul) to the ground, while Saul was on his way to Damascus, and gave him special instructions.

Abraham's Call

The story of Abraham, told in Genesis, is the first story of calling (if you don't count the story of Noah in which God simply put the man to work at a specific task). And while Abraham's story is one in which God called a man, it is, fundamentally, a story about faith. And that's good because faith (i.e., believing/trusting) is fundamental to our response when God calls us. This is also a story about a journey, and it is true that when we respond to God's call, we begin a journey of faith. Christians may ask one another, "How are you doing on the journey?" Sometimes we refer to it as a pilgrimage. And we allude to the fact that this world is not our home; we're just passing through on the way to heaven, which is the promised land. That metaphor had its beginning, of course, in the story of Abraham. God gave him a land for his offspring. The geographical name of that land is Canaan, but God often refers to it as a "land flowing with milk and honey" (Exod. 3:17). For us that land is heaven, something to look forward to, a land where God will wipe every tear from our eyes, and there will be no more death or mourning or crying or pain (Rev. 21:4).

When God calls us to himself, he calls us to trust him as he leads us on the earthly journey to that promised land. We haven't reached that land. Your career is not an end in itself. It is only a small step on the way. You may go into the entertainment field or into medicine or social work or writing and thoroughly enjoy what you do. God may give you a wonderful family and a successful career, the comfort of life and good health and faithful friends, but he doesn't intend for you to get so comfortable that you forget the land that he has promised you some day. This land is temporary. I can think of several friends who have recently recovered from bouts with cancer, and the experience has sharpened their focus on what is important and what is not important in life. The threat of death does that. When we're young, it's easy to live like we're going to live forever. God's call to us is to a life with him in the relatively short time we live in this fallen world, but he also calls us to eternal life in the promised land.

Also note that Abraham left behind everything—friends, some of his family, and a place where he was comfortable. That often happens to us. Responding to God's call sometimes means following a different path than those we have followed before. Family and friends who are not believers can't understand why we don't live the way we used to, why we have new practices, new values, and new goals for life.

Looking to the future for promises to be fulfilled, in faith Abraham believed God. He trusted God, so he packed his tent and his family and everything he owned and set out, having no idea where he was going. However, when God told Abraham that Sarah, his wife, would bear a child, Abraham fell over laughing. He was one hundred years old and found it hard to believe. So we see that while God showed favor with Abraham because of his faith, Abraham wasn't perfect. Like us his faith wavered at times. God chose to work through an imperfect vessel to create his people, and he continues to do that today.

God clearly pointed out to me many years ago that he had given me a gift of writing because he wanted me to use it for him. But I can't count the times over the years when I have sat and stared at blank paper or looked at the sales report of a book which hardly sold more than a few copies and wondered if God really did call me to this work. Perhaps I was supposed to be an electrician or a printer, as I had once contemplated. Then at times, in his mercy, he would show me how some writing of mine had touched someone's life, how he had used it along the way to guide or encourage some struggling soul. And so my flagging faith was revived. And that's how the journey goes and will continue to go.

And so it is with you. You may or may not have a good grasp of your weaknesses as well as your strengths but God does, and he will use you as a broken vessel—a "cracked pot" on the journey that he has planned for you. But know now, as you begin that journey, that it is a journey of faith. The Bible tells us that "Abraham believed God, and it was credited to him for righteousness" (Rom. 4:3).

Abraham's call was more than a call to physically pick up his tent and move. It was a call to believe God, to trust him, to be his servant. We see that emerge later when God calls him to go and climb a mountain (Gen. 22) and sacrifice his only son, Isaac, whom God had given him in his old age. By this time Abraham trusted God enough, so that he got up early the next morning and began to travel. The Bible doesn't record any argument or procrastination. This old man was ready to trust and obey his God. Isaac was the child through whom, God had told him, he would fulfill his promise to make a mighty nation of him and to bless all the world. Such faith is beyond my comprehension. Right up until the last minute, until God directed Abraham's attention to a ram entangled in the bushes, Abraham was ready to obey God and sacrifice his son.

The story is important to us because when God calls us he calls us to a life of faith. Against all hope, the Scripture tells us (Rom. 4:18), Abraham believed God and Abraham's faith was credited to him as "righteousness." That's exactly what happens to us when we answer God's call and believe in him. Our faith in him—our trust, our love—is what God is looking for, and when we believe him and put our trust in him, he places the righteousness of his Son Jesus Christ on us, even though we have done nothing to deserve it. What he asks is that we believe and follow him in this life of faith.

Connecting Art with God: Malcolm's Story

God called Malcolm Hughes by placing him in the middle of a world of art. His father did some painting, but he also sold art, and Malcolm was exposed to good art—mostly what was styled "realism," the world as it is. Malcolm says he began to take Christianity seriously when he was about nine years old, but he learned quickly that the world of art and nature and the world of faith, at least as he had experienced it, didn't connect. The church never talked about art and nature, and those who loved art never talked about faith. So when Malcolm first began painting, he thought that to make his work Christian it had to overtly contain some Christian symbol or even a Bible verse.

Some thinkers believe that the Reformation robbed Protestants of art. When the followers of Luther and Calvin threw out the Catholic doctrine of salvation by works, they also threw out the statues and icons and art in the churches that sometimes replaced God as a focus of worship. In his book *Walk On—the Spiritual Journey of U2,* Steve Stockman tells about the Catholic boy in Northern Ireland who was given a tour of a Presbyterian church as part of a reconciliation program. Noticing how barren it was, he cried out, "You've been robbed."[1] Compared with his church, it was empty, dull, and drab.

Malcolm Hughes is one of those people who is trying to use art—in his case, painting—to speak to our culture without falling into the trap of trying to stamp his art "Christian" with some overt symbols. His art is Christian because it reflects God in his creation.

Not until he was in his teens and began to read the works of a Christian thinker named Francis Schaeffer did Malcolm discover this was a false dichotomy. Schaeffer taught that God is God over all of creation, but we tend to divide the world and life around us into superficial categories such as sacred and secular. Malcolm wanted to be a faithful disciple, and when he understood this, it freed him to become an artist, primarily painting landscapes. Like Schaeffer, Malcolm believes that technology today has tended to remove creation and creativity from us and that we need to regain it. Malcolm has a burning passion to express what he sees in God's creation—the beauty of a sunset or something in the shape of a tree, for example.

So he began taking night courses as a teenager. Then he got a degree in commercial art because it seemed like the best way at the time to get an understanding of the materials and tools of an artist. Next he went off to Europe, and while he worked in the art department for a Christian ministry in Switzerland, he made forays around Europe visiting museums and studying paintings.

Today, Malcolm earns a modest living painting the world as he sees it and trying to communicate what he thinks is true and worthy of attention. At the same time he wants to reconnect those who see his work with God's world. Malcolm believes that there is such a strong focus in some churches on making God the focus of our lives, that it implies that we can't love creation as well.

"There is a real sense of discovery," he says, "in presenting the world as I find it—the shape or color of a particular sky or the way the light comes through in the morning. There are so many amazing things in the natural world. I feel that my role is to help connect people to nature in a time in which the culture has disconnected them. So landscape painting is an expression of my love for God as a creator. The two don't need to compete with each other. For example, when God gave Adam a wife, Adam didn't say, 'Thanks, but I love only you.' On the other hand if we love creation too much, it will lead us away from God."

Esther: The Right Time and Place

Each call is unique. God tailors the call to the person. So God called Esther, a stunningly beautiful young Jewish woman who lived with her cousin, Mordecai, at the time of King Xerxes of Persia. One day the king threw a mammoth party that lasted seven days, and during the party he called for his queen, Vashti, to appear so that all the partygoers could see how beautiful she was. Vashti refused to appear, however, and that really ticked off Xerxes. He turned to his advisors who told him he should find a new queen because Vashti's example was not good for the women of the kingdom. So the most beautiful young women in the kingdom were gathered together, and in time Esther was chosen as the queen and Mordecai was made one of the palace gatekeepers. However, Esther, under Mordecai's direction, did not reveal that she was a Jew.

Meanwhile several of the king's advisors plotted to overthrow him, and Mordecai overheard them. He reported it to Esther who told the king, and when the king investigated and learned that it was true, the plotters were put to death.

Shortly after that, Xerxes made Haman his second in command, a sort of senior administrator of the kingdom. Haman had a big ego and ordered all the people to bow down to him when he passed by, but Mordecai refused to bow down to anyone except God. This infuriated Haman, who persuaded the king to order a decree that on a certain day all the Jews were to be slaughtered. When Mordecai heard this, he instructed Esther to go to the king and ask him to intercede. Esther was taking her life in her hands to do this because anyone who came before the king without his invitation was subject to death. Meanwhile, Haman had erected a gallows on which he planned to hang Mordecai.

One night the king couldn't sleep so he had his servants begin to read the official history of the kingdom. When they came to the account of the king's life being saved by Mordecai, he learned that nothing had been done to reward this man who had done such a great service. So without telling Haman who he was talking about, Xerxes asked Haman what should be done to reward someone who had served the king so faithfully. Haman, with his big ego, thought the king was talking about him and suggested many high honors for this person. But when the king instructed him to carry these out, he learned that Xerxes was talking about Mordecai.

In the end, Mordecai is raised up and Haman is hung on the gallows prepared for Mordecai, and the Jews are delivered because Esther was in the right place at the right time and willing to serve God.

The Right Man at the Right Time: Ron's Story

Just as God called Esther for a special time in history, so God prepared Ron Sykes and called him for a special task at a special time. Ron was a native of Memphis, Tennessee, and had studied first at Union University in Jackson, Tennessee, where he had a personal experience with God and learned that going to church and Christianity were not necessarily the same thing. Ron soon transferred to Memphis State to make it easier on his parents. After graduation he began a career in education, soon moving into administration at private schools. It wasn't always easy. At one school in Natchez, Mississippi, he and his wife, Jane, were thrown into a social whirl that made them very uncomfortable. As the headmaster he was expected to attend a lot of functions where there was heavy drinking. Without knowing where he would go next, he resigned, and the next year found himself in the unlikely position of academic dean at a military school in Virginia. He was given the rank of colonel and had to wear a uniform every day. It was the last place he expected to be but was convinced that for some reason this was the next step in the Lord's plan for him. While the headmaster was traveling and raising funds, Ron found himself running the school day to day and learning a lot about leadership.

Then someone told him about Covenant School—a private Christian school in Charlottesville, Virginia, that was born with a well-thought-through philosophy of integrating faith and learning, Christianity and academics. Now, however, they were struggling with the outworking of that philosophy and looking for a new headmaster. Ron sent his résumé and they sent him an application. "It was the most detailed application I have ever seen," he recalls. "They asked me my philosophy of education, and I was honest. I told them that I thought the Christian school movement had an agenda that was hurting kids rather than drawing them to the Lord. And while I saw Covenant as a place I could have an impact, I really didn't expect them to contact me again.

"The second time I visited it was obvious to me, and apparently to the Covenant board, that this was a match that had been thirty years in the making." Covenant was trying to find out what it looked like to integrate faith and learning. Specifically what did faith look like in the administration of a Christian school. Was it simply a creed and a list of rules? Where did grace come into the picture? As Ron and the Covenant school board talked, they each liked what they heard. Ron fell in love with a board that said, "We're not a church; we're not a Sunday school. We want to be an outstanding academic institution. We do agree on five major tenets of the Christian faith, but we don't have to agree on every rule of behavior."

Ron saw that Covenant was in danger of becoming only another Christian school that says "If you follow the rules and regulations, you'll be a good Christian kid." "It's very important for me," says Ron, "to say, for example, that a violation of the dress code is not a spiritual event. The rules and regulations are important because they say something about who we are, but they don't say anything about our relationship with Jesus Christ. The punk-looking kid out there with the funny hairdo and black shirt can be as solid as the kid who is dressed just to please me."

I'd like to stretch the application of the Esther story here. The nation of Israel was in danger of annihilation when God placed Esther in that influential spot. Here he demonstrated his care and his ability to protect what is his. At this point in history, rather than let the Covenant School slide downhill to become just another school with a creed, God had the right man ready at the right time. Ron says, "Every day I realize that this is exactly where God wants me and that I am in his will. God made me for this place at this time. It took thirty years of following and trusting, and now I understand why."

The Christian life is not only a journey; it is a process in which God continues to shape us into his image. He's not finished with any of us yet and won't be until we are with him and he has made us completely in his image.

From all this, and from the stories that follow in this book, it should be clear that each calling is unique. Calling comes to everyone in a different way. For some it will come through outside voices and events. For others it will come out of deep internal desires and longings. We need to be listening and thinking about calling and asking ourselves what God is trying to tell us.

To Ask Yourself and Others

1. Find several examples in the Bible (other than the ones we've already cited) that show how God called someone to himself or to a specific task.
2. Can you think of someone you know, or know about, who appears to be in exactly the right place at this time for a job that needs to be done? Tell about that person and how you see him or her filling this special need.
3. Has your life's journey so far required you to follow God in faith? Describe that!

Part 2

A Handful from the Saltshaker

One American pastor put it this way: "The call of Jesus on our lives is so huge that it is secondary whether someone fills that as an attorney or as a bi-vocational pastor or as a physician or a homemaker."[1] And while he is right, God, in his wisdom and grace, has ordained that we take our places in his world in various positions, ranging from what we often think of as less important jobs—cleaning, maintenance, construction, simply manual labor—to what we think of as more important jobs in the church and community as leaders, business owners, educators, and so forth.

He didn't stop giving gifts and calling people to serve him at the end of New Testament times. Down through the ages he has used believers and unbelievers to accomplish his purposes. Galileo, for example, besides proving that the earth was not the center of the universe, invented the microscope and built the first telescope. Johannes Gutenberg served God as he invented moveable type, making it possible to print multiple copies of the Bible.

Rembrandt Harmenzoon van Rijn, gave us, among other great works of art, rich scenes of biblical events which add to our grasp of scriptural truths. Thomas Jefferson, John Adams, Benjamin Franklin, and other leaders of the American revolution contributed immeasurably to the freedom of generations of Americans. Jonas Salk discovered a vaccine to prevent a crippling disease and was dubbed, "the man who saved children." Martin Luther King led his generation to stand against a cruel system of racial discrimination and changed the lives and fortunes of tens of thousands of African-American men and women. All of these men, whether they acknowledged it or not, received their gifts from God for the purpose of making this world a better place.

Most of us won't accomplish deeds of this magnitude, nor does God intend us to. Nor does he see a hierarchy in the value of these tasks and accomplishments. Bus drivers and clerks at the convenience store can serve God as well as city councilors and heads of *Fortune 500* companies. It is not the end result of the work that gives it value, it is simply that God had declared that we are serving him, so, no matter what the task—cleaning out a stable or writing a book on nuclear physics—we are to do it with all our hearts as an offering to God.

"Work," wrote British clergyman John Stott, "is the expenditure of energy (manual or mental or both) in the service of others, which brings fulfillment to the worker, benefit to the community and glory to God."[2]

We are called, as the Scriptures tell us, to be the salt of the earth. The analogy breaks down, however, when we consider that, at least to our eyes, each grain of salt looks the same. For not only do we differ in our looks and our makeup but in the ways God has called us to serve. This section contains stories of men and women whom God called to a variety of tasks including architecture, medicine, business, science, and counseling. We've also gone to the

Scriptures for examples of men and women to whom God gave gifts, then called them to use those gifts for him. Each one of our contemporary examples can clearly trace the way God called them to their task, and each one has a clear sense of serving God on the job. Only a few of them have any direct spiritual ministry to the people they come in contact with, except to demonstrate God's love in how they work and relate to others. They serve God more by being the best they can in their work.

CHAPTER 5

The Nature of God's Call

Go to your favorite search engine on the Internet again, and this time type in "God's calling." You'll get a lot of entries, but at least nine out of ten will refer to God calling a pastor or priest or missionary or some other form of church worker. None of the first fifty I checked had any reference to being called to serve God in the marketplace. It simply does not enter the thinking of the average Christian that God calls people to the building trades or teaching or accounting or music or anything outside of the church.

And this misconception is true across the spectrum of Christian traditions—Protestant and Catholic. Both distort the concept of calling and not only apply it primarily to church-related vocations, but they compound the distortion by elevating the church-related vocation over those of the marketplace. I like the way Helen Shoemaker put it:

> We often behave as if God were interested in religion but not in life—in what goes on in church, but not what goes on in a mill or a farm or a broker's office. This point of view overlooks something. It forgets that Christianity began not when religion got carried up farther in the skies, but precisely when it was brought down to earth. It has often been called the most materialistic of all religions because it is constantly

> concerned not with a God in the skies, but with a God who came to earth and lived here. . . . Jesus coming into the world has forever banished the idea of the incompatibility of material with spiritual things.[1]

The fact is it takes many interests, gifts, and skills to make our world work. Consider for a moment the complexity of our society, the technology that makes it go around, the relationships that are built in as a necessary part of our civilization, and the economic framework we've built to provide both our needs and our comforts. It doesn't take much imagination to see that without a wide variety of abilities to keep our system working, we'd soon have a catastrophic breakdown. And on further reflection we realize that God has placed these interests and abilities in people all over the world to bring our world to the advanced state into which we live. We don't give much thought to it, but it is God in his wisdom who sustains this process.

And not only does he equip men and women and call them to many vocations, but no calling is the same. The calling fits the person and his unique circumstances. Thus, my calling, while in college, to a life of writing, editing, and publishing has had no resemblance to that of my friends who have been called to business or building or law or nursing.

Samuel: Hearing God's Unique Call

The Bible is filled with stories not only of God equipping men and women to serve him in various vocations, but of the unique ways in which he called them. No two calls are alike. One of my favorites is the story of Samuel (see 1 Sam. 3). While he was a young boy, Samuel's mother had given him to the priest, Eli, to help in the temple. One night while Samuel was sleeping in the temple near the Ark of God, he heard a voice call his name. Samuel jumped up and ran to Eli and said, "Here I am. What do you need?" (Eli was getting old and was almost blind.) Eli said to Samuel, "I didn't call you. Go back to bed." So the boy went back to bed and again he heard the voice, "Samuel, Samuel." So, again he ran to Eli and said, "I'm here. What do you need?" And, again, Eli told him, "I didn't call you. Go back to bed." When it happened the third time, Eli told Samuel, "Go and lie down, and if you hear the voice again, answer and say, 'Yes, Lord, your servant is listening.'"

So that's what Samuel did and when he answered, the Lord said to him, "I am going to do a shocking thing in Israel. I am going to carry out all my threats against Eli and his family. I have warned him continually that judgment is coming for his family because his sons are blaspheming God, and he hasn't disciplined them. So I have vowed that they will never be forgiven by sacrifices or offerings."

In time, when Eli died, Samuel became the high priest of the people of Israel, and God had a specific job for him to do. The Israelites had persisted in asking God for a king, so it fell to Samuel to anoint Saul, even though he had warned the people of how a king would treat them. Saul, it turned out, did not trust God, and the Spirit of the Lord left him, so God used Samuel to find a shepherd boy, David, and anoint him king to succeed Saul. David turned out to become a man after God's own heart (Acts 13:22). He also wrote many of the beautiful psalms that we quote so often, and God chose David's family line into which Jesus would be born many generations later.

The Bible doesn't tell us specifically why God chose Samuel for this special task, nor what special gifts Samuel had for the job. He simply called Samuel to serve him.

Moses: Using God-Given Abilities

In the same way, I believe, God doesn't choose us to serve him because we have a lot to offer him. The truth is, of course, that we have nothing to offer that he hasn't given us in the first place. Take Moses, for example. He was one of those big-picture people. God gave him leadership skills as well as vision and the ability to see long range how the pieces would come together. The story takes place during the time that the Israelites had become slaves in Egypt and Pharaoh wouldn't let them leave. Moses, the son of a Jewish woman, had been raised in the palace by Pharaoh's daughter (read Exod. 2 to see how this unlikely event occurred), and God called him in one of the most bizarre stories in the Bible.

Moses was out in the field taking care of the flocks of his father-in-law, Jethro, when he noticed a bush burning. The odd thing was that while the flames were coming out of the bush, the fire wasn't consuming the bush. When Moses walked a little closer to investigate, God spoke to him from the bush.

> "Do not come closer," He said. "Take your sandals off your feet, for the place where you are standing is holy ground." Then He continued, "I am the God of your father, the God of Abraham, the God of Isaac, and the God of Jacob." Moses hid his face because he was afraid to look at God. Then the LORD said, "I have observed the misery of My people in Egypt, and have heard them crying out because of their oppressors, and I know about their sufferings. I have come down to rescue them from the power of the Egyptians and to bring them from that land to a good and spacious land, a land flowing with milk and honey . . . . The Israelites' cry for help has come to Me, and I have also seen the way the Egyptians are oppressing them. Therefore, go. I am sending you to Pharaoh so that you may lead My people, the Israelites, out of Egypt." (Exod. 3:5–10)

Moses answered God the same way that I would have answered: "Why me, Lord?" plus several other objections. Moses' leadership skills didn't suddenly pop up. At first he objected to the job. But the Lord met all of Moses' objections with a demonstration of his power (as if the burning bush and his voice weren't enough) by turning Moses' staff into a snake—and then back into a staff.

So Moses went off to do as God said, and it took a lot of courage and trust in God to march back into Pharaoh's palace where he had been brought up and tell this man that God wanted him to let these slaves go. You probably remember the story from Sunday school. Pharaoh wouldn't listen to Moses (it's a wonder he didn't lock him up), but when he saw the people of Israel slacking off in their work, he made life even harder for them. When Moses repeated God's demand and Pharaoh still refused, God sent ten terrible plagues down on Egypt. Each time Pharaoh relented and promised Moses he would let the people go, but then he changed his mind.

Finally, Moses, under God's direction, prepared the people to leave Egypt, and that night God passed over Egypt and struck down the firstborn son in every household in Egypt, except that of the Israelites who had smeared the blood of a lamb on their doorposts. With that, the Bible says, "All the LORD's divisions left Egypt" (Exod. 12:41 NIV).

Moses' work of leadership was far from over, however. For forty years he led the children of Israel through the wilderness. Time and time again this unruly group of people rebelled against Moses and against God, and it called for strong leadership on Moses' part. This chapter isn't about leadership, per se, but it's worth noting that Moses' leadership amounted to turning to God for help, which says a lot about the leadership we need in our day.

The Disciples: A Call to Follow

While God gave Moses the skills of leadership and of looking ahead to see the final goal—the land of milk and honey he had first promised Abraham—sometimes the gifts he gives us or what he wants us to do in the work of the kingdom is not quite so obvious. Take, for example, the fishermen Peter, Andrew, James, and John. Would you have picked them out to be part of your team? The Bible tells us nothing about them except that they were sitting in their boats mending their nets. And when Jesus called them, he didn't give them a job description. He simply said, "I will show you how to fish for people." He said nothing about traipsing up and down the Holy Land for three years, nothing about the sights they would see, about healing people or the miracles they'd witness or eventually perform, nothing about what would happen to him and to them in due time. He simply called them to himself—to follow him. And that's what he does to us. The primary call, as we've said, is to Jesus. He calls us to himself first. Then, and only then, will the details begin to make themselves clear.

Nor is God's primary call related to place. We take the Bible passage, "Go, therefore, and make disciples of all nations" (Matt. 28:19), and emphasize the "go." But the passage may be translated, "Wherever you go in the world, make disciples." We don't have to travel to respond to God's call. Travel is so common in our day, and it's so easy for us to visit the far corners of the earth that we think, for some reason, to respond to God's call we need an American Express Gold card. The first Christians didn't travel. They began church in their own neighborhood.

I received a letter from a friend not too long ago who was paraphrasing the preacher Oswald Chambers. "Never allow yourself this thought," she wrote, "that I am of no use where I am because you certainly can't be used where you haven't been placed." The point is that God doesn't call us primarily to do something but to be something. He calls us to himself and to be like him.

Peter and Andrew and James and John were simply going about their daily tasks when Jesus called them. They had no warning. This happens often to people because it is the Spirit who goes to work in our hearts to draw us to himself when he's ready to do it. Sometimes the Spirit nudges and prepares the hearts of those he calls ahead of time. But often it is right out of the blue.

God's secondary call is more often to a specific task and a specific location, and at times it comes without warning. He called David Turner back into business with little warning; and he put Ron Sykes in the place he had prepared for him and Ron didn't even know what had happened until later on. He moved Tripp Curtiss into the tree business with little notice, and suddenly he opened the door to a new opportunity for Ward Anderson.

Are You Listening?

And that brings up the topic of "listening." As a small boy I lived in a neighborhood in which I had many playmates. Whichever way I went up or down the street, there was Lenny or Richard or David or Charlie. Someone was out and ready to play, just about anytime I was ready.

Often my mother would caution me, "Don't go so far away that you can't hear me when I call." It may be that dinner would be ready soon, or that the family was going out someplace. Of course, I often did go too far. We had one special place to play ball, an old pasture, full of rocks and cow patties (they made excellent bases to tag), but it was far beyond the reach of my mother's voice, which, I believed at the time, was the loudest in the neighborhood. I can't remember ever missing a meal, but I occasionally had to endure her wrath because I strayed too far.

I don't want to press this analogy too far, but I believe one reason many Christians don't hear God's call is that they have wandered too far away. They're involved in pursuits that please them at the moment and they're not listening, not paying attention to what God is saying. Unless we're listening, expecting God to call, we may not recognize his voice when he does speak. Just as I removed myself from the place where I could hear my mother's voice, believers get preoccupied with other things that take them away from the place where they can clearly hear God.

The speed and busy-ness of our lives in our culture also hinders us from hearing God's voice. The Scripture says, "Be still, and know that I am God," but when we're traveling 65 mph on the interstate or rushing from one activity to the next or dashing to the mall to meet friends, then to soccer practice, then home to dinner, it's hard to practice this command. We've programmed meditation and listening time right out of our schedules. How many people have blocked off time in their weekly calendar to do nothing else except listen to God?

The preoccupation with making money or just plain making a living keeps many from stopping to listen. It's true that it often takes a lot of time and hard work to make enough money to get by. And making money for the express purpose of advancing the kingdom of God is a legitimate goal. The problem with wealth, however, is that when we have a lot, it takes more time to look after it and we have more to worry about and more to lose. Anything that demands our time and attention and that we believe will bring some satisfaction to our lives may easily become an idol. An idol is anything we look to before God for satisfaction—sports, hanging out with friends, television, our appearance, our performance. We continually generate these idols, and, if we're honest, we realize that they are the most important things in our lives. Whatever you attempt to draw life and satisfaction from, if it's not God, then it is an idol, and this idol will keep you from hearing God's call on your life.

On the other hand, God spoke so loudly and clearly to the apostle Paul that he couldn't escape. Paul's name was Saul before he met God, and he was having Christians arrested and dragged out of their homes and put in jail. He was traveling to Damascus to do this when a bright light appeared, and it was so strong it knocked him down. At the same time he heard a voice say, "Saul, Saul, why are you persecuting Me?" (Acts 9:4). It was Jesus, and he told Saul to go into Damascus and wait until someone told him what to do.

Every once in awhile I hear about someone who claims that God has spoken to them aloud, and it may very well be true. I have no doubt that the Lord can do that if he wants. However, it seems that this is an exception rather than a rule today. God uses many means—the Scripture, the Holy Spirit, friends, preachers, circumstances, common sense, whatever, to call us and make his will clear to us. I often wonder, however, if we did hear God's voice audibly calling us or telling us what to do, would we be any less resistant to it? I doubt it. The resistance comes from our hearts, not because we don't hear.

Paul is not the only one who resisted God's call. The famous nineteenth-century English preacher Charles Spurgeon wrote, "I must confess I never would have been saved if I could have helped it. As long as I could, I rebelled and struggled against God. When he would have me pray, I would not pray. When he would have me listen to the sound of the ministry, I would not listen. And when I listened and the tear rolled down my cheek, I wiped it away and defied him to melt my heart. Then he gave me the effectual blow of grace, and there was no resisting that irresistible effort."[2]

To Ask Yourself and Others

1. What is in your life that can keep you from hearing God call to you?
2. What other stories of God calling people can you find in the Bible?
3. Are you aware of God calling you to himself? Can you describe the experience?

CHAPTER 6

A Call to Serve

The big decisions about vocation often, but not always, come during the college years and just beyond. For Brian Wispelwey, the primary call, to Christ himself, came early. He certainly couldn't escape hearing it. He was born and brought up in a Dutch ghetto in Prospect Park, New Jersey. Immigrants from the Dutch Reformed church had settled in this small area and completely dominated it. Some 95 percent of the fifty-five hundred residents were of Dutch background and married within the Dutch Reformed church. When Brian's father broke the mold and married an English Episcopalian, Brian's grandfather almost refused to go to the wedding. The social climate was very conservative and strict, and these folks believed strongly in sending their children to their own Christian schools. Here and at home Brian heard and absorbed the idea of faith in Christ, and it became part of him, like breathing in and out.

With their Calvinist background and with the teaching of the Dutch theologian/statesmen Abraham Kuyper practically written on their foreheads, these immigrants believed that all of life came under Christ's dominion. They had rejected the secular/sacred divide that still confuses so many Christians. Everything is sacred they believed, so when some well-intentioned advisors tried to direct Brian into church ministry, Brian's father told him that he could serve God in many ways, and that he was gifted in the sciences. And indeed he was! He majored in biology, and when he graduated he was accepted into a Ph.D. program in biology at Purdue University in Indiana. Once into the program, however, he began asking questions of the professors such as what do you do as a biologist with a Ph.D. One told him you write grant proposals to keep the money flowing so that you can do research. Another told him, "I'm working on something that only five other people in the world care about." Brian realized that he was not wired that way, and a wise professor encouraged him to go into medicine. So Brian finished his work with a master's degree, then went back to New Jersey and enrolled in medical school.

It was clearly the right choice. "On any given day," he says now, "I can say that I helped someone. All jobs are equal in God's eyes, but in some, like medicine, there is more immediacy in seeing how it serves God's creation." In some fields, like business or politics, for example, it takes a little more sorting out and thinking through how what you are doing is more than acquiring wealth or power or doing something that makes you feel good. Brian had a clear sense of wanting to serve although he did not sit down and map out his route into his present vocation. This is the case more often than not. God provides. He moves around the pieces and the people and the circumstances to guide us into the place he wants us.

Medical school students spend a lot of time thinking about what area they want to specialize in. For Brian it was internal medicine, but he also liked the sub-specialty of infectious diseases. So he and his wife, Bev, and their son, Seth, went off to Boston for Brian's residency with the Harvard University system.

The AIDS epidemic was just appearing on the horizon when Brian was in Boston, and while San Francisco, Los Angeles, and New York were the centers of AIDS work, Boston was not far behind, and he began working with some of the leading investigators in the field. He had his first AIDS patient in 1981, and was soon involved in a cutting-edge and exciting area of medicine. It was intellectually scary, he remembers. "I had all kinds of emotions. People were running from this disease. The social and ethical issues made your head spin. Also, the fact that people weren't lining up to get into this area of medicine gave it some appeal for me."

People asked Brian, "Why do you want to do this? You're wasting your life. These people got what they deserved." (When the epidemic broke out, the majority of cases were gay men.) "Sooner or later, they warned me, you're going to get this disease." And the more they questioned and warned him, the stiffer his resolve became to go into this frontier area of medicine with all its unknowns.

Meanwhile he had begun to apply for fellowships in infectious diseases, and when the University of Virginia offered him a fellowship, he decided to go. It wasn't the center of infectious disease research, but it would give him some personal leeway in what he wanted to do. As it turned out, when a few AIDS cases showed up, because of his Boston experience and because no one else there had any experience in the field, they asked him to set up a department of infectious diseases. "It's interesting," he observes. "My entire medical career of twenty-two years parallels the onslaught of this disease."

As a whole, evangelical churches, with some notable exceptions, have turned their backs on this area of need and often refused to accept people with AIDS into their churches. As a Christian physician, Brian has had to swim upstream at times. A woman in his church once came to him for help in organizing the church members to do something in their community to help victims of AIDS. She put a notice in the church bulletin about a meeting and convinced Brian to say something. On the appointed evening, he and the woman waited and waited but no one came. Another time the church had a meeting for the many health care professionals that attend that church to interest them in short-term medical missions. Close to two hundred people attended the meeting, and a visiting missionary doctor told how he saw the face of God in his patients. Brian stood up and said something to the effect that we have all these people ready to go across oceans to see the face of Jesus in people in need, but we can't get anyone to go two blocks away to see that. "Shouldn't medical missions begin at home?" he challenged them.

Part of Brian's mentality as a Christian, instilled in him by his father and his grandfather, is that we're not in this world only for ourselves. We have a responsibility beyond ourselves. Again, this service outlook stems from a Christian worldview that says that Christ is in all aspects of our culture.

For the Sake of Economic Justice

Ron Gilbert came to this point of view in an entirely different way. His upbringing had little in common with Brian's except for caring, attentive parents. Ron was brought up in the Catholic church in a family of German and French. His dad set up the accounting system for the Air Force Academy in Colorado, in the early days of computers, so Ron was exposed to the military and to flying. He decided that that's what he wanted to do, but, sadly, learned that he was color blind and needed glasses. So he attended the Coast Guard Academy, but left after two years and never did take a flying lesson. He transferred to the University of Virginia and began studying engineering and soon discovered he wasn't cut out for that either. With the next level of calculus staring him in the face, he transferred to the McIntire School of Commerce and majored in finance and marketing and found his calling.

He began selling insurance while in college and after graduation went off to Boston to work in the home office of the New England Life Insurance Co., while he took graduate work at the

American College at Bryn Mawr, Pennsylvania, through a distance learning program. Insurance agreed with him, and he eventually took a position in San Francisco with one of the largest insurance companies in the country. When that company ran into serious financial trouble, Ron stumbled, providentially, he believes, into what has become his passion for the last twenty-five years. He went to work for a man named Louis Kelso, who told Mike Wallace on *60 Minutes* that "Americans are a nation of industrial sharecroppers who work for someone else and have no other source of income. If a man owns something that will produce a second income, he'll be a better customer for the things that American industry produces. But the problem is how to get the working man that second income."

Kelso also told President Gerald Ford at the time that proposals for more tax cuts and more welfare will never solve the economic mess we're in. "They don't go to the root of the problem."

Kelso's idea was simple: give workers a share in the ownership of the company they work for, so Kelso came alongside of companies and helped them set up plans whereby employees could own stock in the company. It's called an ESOP, Employee Stock Ownership Plan, and works for both private and publicly owned companies. It benefits companies by increasing their net worth, giving them substantial tax savings, and increasing their cash flow. It benefits employees by giving them a direct share in the growth of the company and receiving larger benefits than they'd normally receive through other types of retirement plans. It has also proven to be an employee motivator, building both unity and team spirit. The idea appealed to Ron because of the service dimension of it. He saw himself helping thousands of economically disenfranchised people get a larger share in the benefits of their labors. However, the laws regulating business made it complicated for a company to convert to this type of ownership, so the Kelso

Company served as consultants, helping companies through the conversion process.

Both Ron and Sue had responded to Christ's call on their lives in 1976 while living in Kansas City, just before they moved to San Francisco. Ron had been reluctant to make the commitment because he was convinced that as soon as he did, someone was going to call him and say, "We want you to go to Africa to become a missionary." Still, with Sue prodding him, he made the commitment to Christ.

There was a lot of renewal going on in the Catholic church at that time, and Ron and Sue got involved in Bible studies wherever they lived. They began to listen to a Christian television broadcast, and Ron, knowing he had gifts in marketing and finance, called the broadcasters and asked if he could help them. He had a deep desire to be involved in some kind of ministry. He remembers clearly now that the man he talked to asked him if he was having some kind of a problem. When Ron said no, the man told him that's good because many people think they can get away from their problem by getting involved in some ministry, and "if you get involved with us," he told Ron, "you'll have more problems."

While attending the Bible studies in the San Francisco Bay area, both Ron and Sue became convinced that for the sake of their children, they needed to move their family back east. They wanted a small town or country setting where they were apt to find a more wholesome setting for their two (eventually to become four) boys. While on a trip to Washington, D.C., for Kelso & Company, Ron saw an ad for a small farm for sale in Virginia, and it seemed to be exactly what they were looking for. So they prayed, sought the counsel of others and asked others to pray for them, then told the company managers they wanted to move east. Kelso set Ron up as their East Coast representative. When Kelso & Co. decided to move to New York in 1983 and move all their employees there, Ron left the company, and with their blessing, Ron and Sue set up a company called ESOP Services, Inc. Today he sees himself working for economic justice. Louis Kelso, the father of the ESOP, preached that every worker should receive a share of the wealth he helps to produce in proportion to his contribution and that each household should have an opportunity to earn a decent standard of living. Where communism went wrong, he believed, is that it turned to the state to determine the level of each citizen's daily existence, operating on the principle of "from each according to his ability, to each according to his need."

Whether or not we agree with the economic principles and whether or not they work, the point is that what puts the extra energy in Ron's steps as he works is the knowledge that he is bringing a better standard of living to thousands of families.

While there are more than 10,000 companies in the U.S. with ESOPs, and 10 million employee-owners, Ron believes the concept has a bright future. When the Iron Curtain fell and Eastern European countries came out from under the influence of the Soviet Union, these countries began to build a new economic system and most chose varying degrees of free-market capitalism. Ron saw an opportunity to help, and they ventured into countries such as Poland and Lithuania, helping to set up ESOPs. There are now more ESOPs in Poland (approximately 1,000) than anyplace else in the world, except the United States.

Both Brian and Ron have a firm belief that they are serving God by serving people in their work. They go to work each day understanding that they are doing much more than examining patients or studying financial statements. They know that their work contributes to making this world a better place, and often they can see the tangible results. They see what they are doing with a big-picture view of the world.

Serving God by Serving People

This understanding relieves the pressure that many Christians feel to make the workplace a fishing pond for souls. Too often Christians in the workplace believe they have to advertise that they have something others don't—that is, Jesus, and that everyone needs him. Well, everyone does need Jesus, but direct confrontation or uninvited witness of our faith is often not the best way to communicate the gospel and can be counter-productive. That doesn't mean that either Brian or Ron would not tell people about their faith in Christ if the opportunity clearly opened before them. It simply means that they don't feel a strong need to justify their daily existence as a Christian by wearing their Christianity on their sleeve or pushing literature on unsuspecting unbelievers. They are demonstrating their faith day by day in what they do, in the meaning of their work—as well as in how they love people with whom they work.

French philosopher/theologian Jacques Ellul said, "When I became a professor, I discovered that the meaning of my work lay not in the science of transmitting information, but in my relationship with my students."[1] And James Rouse, a builder of many restored neighborhoods in Baltimore wrote, "We are God's instruments for carrying out creation. Therefore the mission of the Christian is to be a co-creator, in human institutions, in human relations, and in nature. In the spirit of co-creators, we should be moved to solve the problems around us."[2] With this kind of view of work, which Brian Wispelwey and Ron Gilbert share, there is no pressure to be an evangelist in the workplace. God has other reasons for them to be there. As they move up in their respective fields, they see it as advancing the kingdom of God, not advancing a career.

Os Guinness tells the story of a small village in France during World War II. The people of Le Chambon rescued more than five thousand Jewish children from the Nazis. When praised for their goodness, they typically responded, "What do you mean by such foolish words as 'good' and 'decent'?" They believed simply that they were doing what had to be done, that it was a natural thing to help people in need. Guinness is trying to make the point that "the call of Jesus is personal, but not purely individual; Jesus summons his followers not only to an individual calling but also to a corporate calling."[3]

All work, I believe is service of some kind. Some work, however, calls for more risk than others. Brian Wispelwey had risked the accident of infection with HIV, even though he takes all necessary precautions. Ron Gilbert takes the risk of running a small business and of having his specialty legislated out of existence.

In Carthage, a city in North Africa, in the third century, a plague broke out. It was a fearful time as the disease spread quickly from house to house. To protect themselves people began to throw the bodies of those who died from the plague out into the street. A group of Christian believers, however, who called themselves the *Parabolani*, went from street to street collecting the bodies for burial, as well as ministering to the sick. The term means "one who takes a risk" and is used to describe the gambler who placed everything he owned on one throw of the dice. It was also the term used by Paul to describe his friend Epaphroditus, who almost died risking his life for Christ (see Phil. 2:30).

All service involves some risk. Any act of reaching out, no matter how small, has its dangers. When we offer friendship we risk rejection. When we give freely of our time and goods, we may be misunderstood. When we commit ourselves to help the homeless and the handicapped, we jeopardize our comfort and, perhaps, our health. William Barclay wrote that in the Christian there should be an "almost reckless courage which makes him ready to gamble with his life to serve God and men."[4] And in a famous meditation

John Donne offers one reason why we take any kind of a risk to serve others: "All mankind is of one author, and is one volume; when one man dies, one chapter is not torn out of the book, but translated into a better language; and every chapter must be so translated. . . . As therefore the bell that rings to a sermon, calls not upon the preacher only, but upon the congregation to come: so this bell calls us all: but how much more me, who am brought so near the door by this sickness. . . . No man is an island, entire of itself . . . any man's death diminishes me, because I am involved in mankind; and therefore never send to know for whom the bell tolls; it tolls for thee."[5]

We tend to see the world moving around us, when it is really moving around God. In any major decision relating to vocation, it is helpful to remind ourselves that it is not about us; it's about God and his kingdom.

Helping people with AIDS and helping people in the workplace improve their economic situation can have a certain amount of glamour attached. But not all service is glorious. The English clergyman/writer John Stott tells about a man walking down a country lane who came across some men working in a stone quarry. He asked them what they were doing, and the first man, looking annoyed, replied "I'm cutting rocks." The second man told him, "I'm making $200 a day." The third man put down his pick, stuck out his chest, and said, "You want to know what I'm doing? I'm building a cathedral." This man was able to see far beyond the specific task and see how that task fit into God's larger plan.

Martin Luther King Jr. put it this way: "If a man is called to be a street sweeper, he should sweep streets even as Michelangelo painted, or Beethoven composed music, or Shakespeare wrote poetry. He should sweep streets so well that all the host of heaven and earth will pause to say, 'Here lived a great street sweeper who did his job well.'"[6]

The Scripture tells us, "And whatever you do, in word or in deed, do everything in the name of the Lord Jesus, giving thanks to God the Father through Him" (Col. 3:17). God's call may mean what appears to some as drudgery. But if we are convinced that this is what he wants us to do, and we do it for God, the commonplace and the menial may take on new meaning. Some are called to leadership and to fame—to high political office or to write best-sellers or head *Fortune 500* companies or lead armies into battle. While others are called to stuff envelopes, sell groceries, work on the production line, or dig trenches.

Several hundred years ago a French priest named Jean-Pierre de Caussade wrote a book called *The Sacrament of the Present Moment*. He argued that "to discover God in the smallest and most ordinary things, as well as in the greatest . . . is to possess a rare and sublime faith."[7] God can instill the meaningless with meaning. He can lend dignity to the mundane. Shuffling papers or maneuvering a front loader or weeding a garden or cleaning toilets and washing diapers can be acts of worship in which God is present when we do it for him. Os Guinness calls this "the splendor of the ordinary."[8]

To Ask Yourself and Others

1. Seeing daily tasks in this wider perspective of fitting into the work of God's kingdom is a good habit to develop. Take some daily task that you are required to do and describe how it fits into God's larger purpose.
2. Name several areas of work you think you might enjoy and describe how they advance the kingdom of God.
3. If you have some specific vocational area that interests you, try to identify what it is that you would find fulfilling in this kind of work. Why would you want to do it?

CHAPTER 7

This I Must Do!

For some of us it takes many years to learn enough about ourselves—our inclinations, gifts, personality, and so on—to know with any certainty the field of work to which God is calling us. For others, it becomes apparent early in life, and the knowledge drives them to do what they just have to do. This describes Amy Sherman perfectly. Amy's passion is to help the poor although the question she has struggled with has always been, "Am I to be involved in direct, hands-on work with the poor, or should I direct my efforts toward changing public policy and mobilizing resources to help the poor?"

Amy was brought up just outside of Buffalo, New York. Her parents divorced when she was in junior high school, and because her older brother and sister had left home, she recalls a childhood of mostly herself and her mother. They lived in a working-class neighborhood, and because money was tight, she worked after school and in the summer for about six years on a farm, picking beans and tomatoes. This gave her an early exposure to poverty through migrant workers.

"Somewhere along the way," she says, "I developed a strong work ethic. I like to work. My mom and the people around me worked hard."

The summer before her eighth grade in school she attended a summer camp, heard the gospel, and committed her life to Christ.

The woman who led her to Jesus had friends in the town next to where Amy lived, and the woman, knowing that her friends had experience discipling new believers, introduced her to Tim and Jan. Eventually she went to spend weekends with them and got involved in their church.

She stayed involved in her own Methodist church, and one summer when she was in junior high school the youth group went to Appalachia to do community service work. In her mind, Amy can still see an old woman living by herself in a miserable old shack way up on a mountain. The shack had no electricity nor running water, so every day the woman took two buckets, walked about a mile downhill to a stream, filled the buckets, and hauled them up the mountain. From that summer on Amy knew that her life was going to have something to do with the intersection of the church and the poor. She has never wavered from this, and she continued to be involved in ministry to the poor, not because she was part of a group and everyone else was doing it but because she wanted to do it. She felt fulfilled in doing it.

From then on, whenever she found an opportunity to be involved in service to the poor she was there. At Messiah College she struggled more with the question of where she should serve—as a Peace Corps worker, for example, or in some other work that would put her in direct contact with the poor, or perhaps she could advance public policy as a lobbyist or a public defender. While her instincts led her to think of direct contact, her counselors in college told her that she had God-given gifts that could be used to help many others help the poor. Also, Amy had had a serious automobile accident while in college that limited her fitness for any strenuous activity, so that suggested to her that indirect involvement might be her role. From that time forth her involvement has leaned from one side to the other.

Early on in college, she had devoted an inordinate amount of time to sports, but with the accident she had to drop that. She sees that now as providential in directing her time toward ministry to the poor. She majored in political science, got involved in student government, and in her senior year became the school chaplain. This meant that she not only had to organize and run the Sunday evening, student-led services, but also organize the annual spring break service project, directing students to both the inner city and to Appalachia.

After graduation from Messiah she took a job in Washington, D.C., with the James Madison Foundation where she worked for a Catholic scholar named George Weigel. Under Weigel she began to learn about Catholic social teaching and about Dorothy Day and the Catholic Worker Movement. "It expanded my understanding as a Christian," she recalls, "of how to think about economics."

In 1989 Amy left D.C. to take graduate work at the University of Virginia, where she had some freedom to design her own program. She ended up concentrating on economic development issues and how religion and culture intersect with economics. She received a Ph.D. from UVA while continuing some hands-on work among the poor as well as trying to motivate and equip others for such ministry. She was one of the first telephone volunteers for a local group called Love Inc. in which she fielded calls from people in need and helped to mobilize local churches to be involved in the lives of these people. She also helped to found a magazine called *Stewardship Journal*, which focused on how Christians should be involved in international development. The magazine began to look at domestic poverty as well, and that stirred Amy's interest in poverty at home.

Meanwhile her local church was beginning to ask how they could reach the poor in their town, and Amy got involved. She established a church-based ministry called Charlottesville Abundant Life Ministries in an inner-city neighborhood.

Today, as a scholar-practitioner, Amy is a senior fellow at the Welfare Policy Center of the Hudson Institute, a Washington, D.C., think tank. This means that she does research and then connects her research to actual ministry to the poor so that it doesn't remain hypothetical.

Looking back she says, "The Lord knew that I'm very impatient, and I didn't want to spend years trying to figure out what I was supposed to do with my life. So in the eighth grade he pointed it out to me, and I'm grateful for the clarity of that call. I tell people today that my call is to equip the saints for ministry among the poor."

Amy's call helps to reinforce the idea that God calls us not so much to a specific place but to service of some specific kind. The biblical passage "Go, therefore, and make disciples of all nations" (Matt. 28:19) may also be translated "wherever you go in the world, make disciples." Too often we emphasize the idea of "going," as though you have to leave home to serve God, even though believers in the early church began right where they were. Amy learned that the poor are everywhere, so it doesn't matter whether she is in Buffalo or Appalachia or Washington, D.C., or Charlottesville, Virginia—she can serve the poor wherever she happens to live and work.

Amy doesn't believe that she has a gift for mercy, but she does believe she is called to implant a vision for mercy and equip those who have the gift. All of us are required to show mercy, but God has planted in the hearts of some an extra measure of concern for the poor, the oppressed, the disenfranchised, and those who are hurting, and he will prepare them and lead them to where they can exercise this gift. Those who are called to mercy ministries have no more merit in God's sight than those called to business or engineering or drama, for example, but they are often—not always—more clearly aware of the results of their ministry.

Amy's concept of calling—that she can use her gifts wherever she is—is similar to the perspective of some people who are "tentmakers." The term is usually applied to people who have gone to a country or culture not as "missionaries" with a church-related agency but earn their living in that culture by working in a profession—engineer, health-care worker, teacher, or whatever. One study of these people found that many who had gone to a country to use their professions as a base for doing missionary work suffered considerable emotional and spiritual trauma. But those whose main reason for living in a foreign country was to practice their profession often became powerful witnesses and servants for Christ. Their "primary calling is to a specific profession, out of which Christian witness flows naturally."[1]

Called to the Secular: Bill's Story

Most of this subhead is a good description of Amy Sherman, the scholar/researcher in poverty and worker among the poor. It also describes a man named Bill Stuntz, a professor at Harvard Law School in Cambridge, Massachusetts. When he was young, Bill had no idea what he wanted to do when he grew up. His father worked in the aerospace industry as an engineer, involved with guided missile systems and high-tech weaponry. That didn't appeal to Bill, and he finally chose William and Mary as a place to study, not for academic reasons but because when he visited he saw more pretty girls on the campus than at other schools. He had a double major of history and English, but realized that didn't help in the job market, so he went off to law school at the University of Virginia. Looking back he says, "I would have said at the time that I was a Christian, but perhaps I wasn't." It seems, at least, that seeking God's will for his life was not part of the decision, and he had no idea whether he'd like law school, nor what kind of law he wanted to practice.

In college and in law school he went to several meetings of Christian organizations but sensed that they were dominated by people who were alienated from their group. "I found a high representation of people unhappy with student life. They felt that college or graduate school was not working for them. I felt these were often support groups for unhappy Christian students. I loved college and I loved law school, so I suspect that if I was a Christian, I was very immature."

In law school Bill and Ruth, whom he had met at William and Mary, attended a small Baptist church where she played the organ and directed the choir. It wasn't until Bill left law school and moved to Philadelphia to clerk for a federal judge that he felt the real tug of the Spirit on his heart. He and Ruth attended the Tenth Presbyterian Church, and Bill responded to the preaching of the pastor, James Boice. "I had never been in a church before where I felt so challenged. Every Sunday the preacher would make you squirm, rather than tell you how good you are and help you feel better about yourself. This preacher would say, 'Let me tell you about yourself'—and it was not an attractive picture."

From there Bill went to Washington, D.C., to clerk for Supreme Court Justice Lewis Powell, and then they moved back to Charlottesville where Bill taught federal criminal law at UVA law school.

He found that he enjoyed this, especially working with students, more outside the class than in. He had been teaching at UVA for five years when Yale University asked him to come for a year and teach. Before a law school will invite a professor for a permanent position, they will invite him to teach for a year as a visiting professor. And while Bill was not especially happy with Yale Law School, he did develop relationships with students that were fulfilling, and he and Ruth found a church they loved. However, Yale never did invite him to come permanently, so they went back to UVA.

Next, Harvard invited him to come and teach for a year, but after the experience with Yale he had low expectations. By this time Bill and Ruth were actively seeking God's will for themselves as they made these career decisions. While thinking about it he remembered a message from his pastor who, in considering his own call to leave for another church, had talked about the intersection of gifts, inclination, and opportunity. And while the Yale experience had not been the best, and they had good friends and a good church in Charlottesville, they both felt they didn't want to get to the end of their lives and realize they had said no to God the one time he had asked them to do something uncomfortable. "I began looking for the writing on the wall telling us what to do," he recalls. It didn't come, so Bill began to pray, "Lord, give me your heart. I want to long for the things you want me to long for. If you want me to pull up stakes here, I want to long for that." And God answered that prayer. Today when he counsels students he tells them to do that and encourages them to pray, "Lord, redeem my mistakes. You're a God who delights to take error and use it." So, while Bill knew that his primary call was to Christ and that God had given him a love of the law as a way of serving him, he also found fulfillment in working with students. "I've felt much more useful here at Harvard," he says. "I've found a much greater need on the part of Christian students for someone to validate them."

For example, he explains, "The biggest need for Christian law students in a place like Harvard is how to think about conventional careers. Most seem to think that if they go out and work for the poor and the oppressed, God will smile on them, but if they go and work in a prosecutor's office, for example, their professional life will be worthless in God's eyes. They think, perhaps they should have gone to seminary and that God smiles only on those in 'ministry.' Most of them will go into conventional law careers, so from the beginning they have a view of calling that insures they'll be alienated and unhappy. It's a destructive message to say to a student that you've got to get with the program and get into some kind of work to help the needy."

To those who wonder how Bill Stuntz fares as an evangelical Christian believer at the notoriously secular Harvard University, he tells them that it's different than they might expect. At Harvard Christians are seen as interesting, a bit of a curiosity. No one is threatened by them so no one is hostile.

Both Amy's and Bill's stories lean against the myth of individualism that many Americans cherish. A myth circulates in our society that we are or can be self-sufficient. We are encouraged to think that we are independent, that we can get on by ourselves and choose the values, the lifestyles, and the path in life that we want to choose. We have made heroes of the frontiersmen who went forth and "made it on their own." We applaud the person who makes good in this world seemingly without help from family, friends, or community. In reality, however, none of us are independent of society. We are all interdependent. We need one another. As Robert Bellah, editor of "Habits of the Heart," argued, people who believe they can meet their own needs form a habit of thinking of themselves in isolation and imagine that their whole destiny is in their hands.

There is not only nothing biblical in that; it is pure nonsense to boot. We live in an enormously interdependent world where what I do—my choices of a career, as well as my daily activities—affect many others, including, probably, you. And when it comes to determining God's calling, we need to keep in mind our relationship to the body of Christ; that is, all Christian believers. As God's secondary calling became clear to Amy and Bill, they recognized that their lives were closely entwined with many others. I have no right to go off in a corner by myself and figure out what God wants me to do. I offend God when I do so by ignoring the help he offers through other believers. We are members of a family and a community. The awareness which both Amy and Bill have of these truths has led them to enormously fruitful and satisfying careers.

Know Your Spiritual Gifts

Another reason why we need to ask the church to help us in determining our call is that we have all been given spiritual gifts for the purpose of serving the body of Christ. The apostle Paul wrote to the Corinthians: "About matters of the spirit, brothers, I do not want you to be unaware. . . . Now there are different gifts, but the same Spirit. There are different ministries, but the same Lord. And there are different activities, but the same God is active in everyone and everything. A manifestation of the Spirit is given to each person to produce what is beneficial" (1 Cor. 12:1–7).

Paul isn't talking here about talents such as a good musical ear or physical ability to kick a ball or dance or visual skills needed to be a landscape painter or manual dexterity. Those are skills God gives us to guide us into some particular field. No, here he is talking about spiritual gifts, the gifts that will help you in the specific kind of *ministry* he wants you involved in no matter what vocational field you are in. A businessman, for example, might have the gift of teaching and/or the gift of mercy. There's a good chance he will also have the gift of giving because he will probably have more opportunity to use that gift than a street sweeper who works for the minimum wage.

Your spiritual gift may also be a guide to the vocational field in which God wants you to work. So, along with determining what skills and aptitudes you have, you also need to seek out what spiritual gifts the Lord has given you. And you may find that you have several spiritual gifts, not only one.

You'll find lists of spiritual gifts in three different places in Paul's writings: Romans 12:6–8; 1 Corinthians 12:1–10; and Ephesians 4:11. (Notice that in Eph. 4:12 Paul emphasizes again the purpose of these gifts: "to build up the body of Christ." That says to me that in determining how I'm going to serve him in whatever field I'm in I need to consult with other believers as part of the body of Christ.)

Among the gifts listed in these passages are exhortation, giving, leadership, prophecy, service, teaching, discernment, administration, faith, healing, mercy, wisdom, hospitality, and evangelism.

To Ask Yourself and Others

1. Who would you go to for counsel in determining whether God is calling you into a specific field or job?
2. What kind of work might you find compelling and something you "just have to do"?
3. Read the passages from Scripture that I've listed above and describe what you feel may be your spiritual gifts. Talk this over with several wise counselors and see what they think.

CHAPTER 8

Do I Have a Choice?

Historians, sociologists, and journalists have a habit of dividing recent history into decades—the thirties, forties, fifties, nineties, and so on. And while it's not realistic to look at these decades as separate and unique, it is true that our culture has changed from decade to decade. Life and the cultural customs and emphases of the thirties are a far cry from that of the sixties, and that infamous generation bears little resemblance to this first decade of the twenty-first century.

Various things account for that change—technology for one; politics for another. My parents knew nothing about television nor international air travel. Television was just coming along when I was in high school, but we never dreamt of computers or video games or cell phones. The young people of every recent generation have faced the possibility of going off to war although those wars and the effect they had on the nation differed greatly. The day after the Japanese bombed Pearl Harbor (Dec. 7, 1941) long lines of young men were outside military recruiting stations to sign up and fight a war. Can you imagine that today? No! Many of those young men, who had grown up in the Great Depression, quit college to go off and risk their lives serving their country. (I told you that generations differ.)

Today our culture assumes that we are on earth to feel good. We work very hard at avoiding any discomfort and finding what philosopher Francis Schaeffer called "personal peace and affluence." When it comes to finding our life's work, this translates into comparing the job benefits as well as the downside of a particular line of work. Those who choose the military as a profession, for example, understand it will impose many limitations on their personal freedom while offering some benefits that other lines of work do not. Entrepreneurs understand that they'll have to live with a larger amount of risk than, say, veterinarians or nutritionists or hair stylists. Doctors usually expect a higher income, thus a higher level of living than those in the building trades, and pilots may be looking for a kind of adventure that will never come to an accountant.

We take a battery of tests to determine what we enjoy doing, what we're gifted for, what type of work our personalities lend themselves to, and in all of this we assume that the world is our playground. We can look it over and pick and choose where we want to play and what we want to play on. The choice is ours.

But in this book we've begun to talk about God preparing us and God calling us to a specific job in a specific place. So we have to stop and ask, "Does God have it all mapped out for us? Do we have any say in the matter? Can we choose what we want to do, or are we reduced to finding out what God wants us to do for him? What about my rights? Do I have any?" Good questions! Let's try and answer them through the lives of several people.

God's Plans Are Best: Katherine's Story

Katherine Leary has been the chief executive of a start-up consulting company in New York City, as well as the head of a dot-com company in Silicon Valley. But if you met her in the supermarket, you might peg her not for a high-powered corporate executive but for a kindly fifth-grade school teacher, which she once was.

Katherine grew up assuming that she should and could do what she wanted to do—the decisions, she believed, were hers to make. As a young girl in South Brunswick, New Jersey, she often rallied the neighborhood kids, including her three younger brothers, into the basement of her home to play school—and, of course, she was the teacher. After college she did teach for two years and worked summers for a firm that was doing consulting for the space program. That seemed to her so much more exciting than teaching, so she took a computer course that was necessary to join this firm and left teaching far behind.

This, she recalls was her first exposure to people who were living for a cause. They were part of the space race. To her colleagues, what they were doing was a religion. Technology was going to change their world, and she became a part of it. She rose quickly, but soon realized she needed more education in the field, so she went to the Darden School at the University of Virginia, one of the country's best business schools, then went to New York City to work for a cutting-edge company, advising other companies how they could improve their communication. If she thought about God or Christianity during those days, it was simply to wonder how intelligent people could fall for all that superstition.

One morning she walked into the office and the president pulled her aside. "I've got bad news," he told her. "I have a brain tumor and need surgery, and I'm leaving in thirty minutes for an operation. If I make it I won't be back for nine months." Katherine ended up running the company but, at the same time, began to think more about God, trying to figure out what and who he was. Meanwhile, her family had become Christian believers, and she noticed many positive changes in their lives. Her own perspective on how the world worked was not holding water, but it took her a long time to admit she was wrong.

One of her employees was part of a group who had begun a church in Manhattan called Redeemer Church, and she persuaded Katherine to go and listen to a man named Tim Keller who spoke at the church. "It was a several-year process," she says now, "but God would not let me go. There was a lot of pride and a lot of lifestyle to give up. My head had to be converted.

"In the end," she recalls now, "there was no moment of, 'Eureka,' when I discovered the truth; it was, instead, a moment of submission that Jesus is who he said he is."

Katherine has good analytical skills, relational skills, and leadership ability, and she began to realize that God had given her these skills for his purposes. She continued to move through the business world, and ended up in Silicon Valley, home of the fast-growing dot-com boom. With the greed and ambition of that period, it often seemed like "pitching her tent at the gates of hell." She found out that the values were so different. "We were in the 'toot your own horn' arena, and there was a lot of arrogance and entitlement around. It was a challenging time, and I was not immune to getting caught up in the excitement. As I struggled I wondered how God was going to compete."

When the company got caught in the dot-com bust, Katherine took a sabbatical. A local church asked her to come on staff and minister to people in the workplace. After a year, Redeemer Church in New York City asked her to return there and begin a program to reach people in business. For Katherine it was less a question at this point of what she wanted to do. She had placed her life in God's hands and wanted to trust him. Her desire to please him overrode the competing desires to remain in Silicon Valley and join another company, earning the big income.

But by now Katherine had learned that when serving Christ

becomes your primary goal in life—when that's what you want to do more than anything else—you don't ask, "Do I have any rights?" When your passion is to call attention to Christ, you lose the desire to map out your own life. You realize that, left up to you, you make a big mess of it. And you know that the one who created you and gave you the gifts, abilities, and experience you have can do a much better job than you can of directing your life. As Katherine said, her conversion experience climaxed in a moment of submission to God's will, which meant giving up her own.

"It's not that what I had been doing had no value," she reflects. "Despite the ups and downs of technology, I feel fortunate that I've been in the kinds of businesses I have been in. These businesses had some significance. They mattered." And that, of course is what attracted her to business. She not only enjoyed the challenge of leading a team and helping people perform well, but when she went home at night, she had a sense of being involved in something that would make the world a better place to live. Now she recognizes that, while she didn't make her career choices with a conscious recognition of pleasing God, he was guiding her life and those choices even back then.

Katherine also experienced what many others have learned—we move around in our careers, not only from one job to another but, for some, from one type of work to another. The day my grandfather graduated from college he went to work for AT&T and worked for the company until he retired. My aunt did likewise for a brokerage firm in Boston. Today, this is highly unusual. In fact, many seminary students today are older men who have worked in some field—business or engineering or the military, for example—and believed God was calling them to serve in the church. There is no particular virtue in staying with one company or even in one discipline or field of work. The point is to be walking close enough to God to hear him if he calls you to some other area of service.

So Katherine Leary, after twenty years in business, responded to a call from Redeemer Church back in New York City where she uses the experience she has in business to help people in their professions develop a sense of mission and see how what they are doing fits into God's plan. Redeemer Church, sitting as it does strategically in the middle of that thriving city, has a strong sense of being part of changing the culture by living as God's people in the middle of it. Katherine is especially qualified to help people do that. God knows what he is doing and has plans for her and for us that we would never ever dream of.

Using God's Gifts: Tom's Story

Tom Miller provides another example of God managing our lives better than we could. Tom is a research scientist with a company called Aton Pharma in New York City. For someone from a blue collar home in southern Indiana who never expected to go to college, he has come a long way. He now has a Ph.D. in bioorganic chemistry, is the holder of several patents for biological discoveries, was awarded "Inventor of the Year" by the University of Virginia, and is a science advisor to major Wall Street banks.

Tom's father spent many years in the Marines, did a lot of fighting in Korea, was gone a lot, and when he was home, he struggled with alcohol. Eventually Tom's parents divorced when he was fifteen.

Tom's older brothers went into the military, but there was no way his mother was going to let him go that route. She was making money in real estate, so after high school Tom began to help her. But, several years out of school, he suddenly realized there is more to life than making money, so he went to the University of Indiana at Bloomington and majored in chemistry. He had always loved school, and he did well at the university. But, along the way he learned that opportunities for someone with a bachelor's degree in chemistry are limited, especially in his small hometown, so, with Carlonna, whom he had married while in college, he went off to Virginia for graduate work at the university.

It was there that he and Carlonna began to look seriously at Christianity. Tom had gone to a Methodist church up until he was about twelve years old, then, when given the option to decide for himself whether he wanted to go, he opted out. In graduate school in Virginia, life was hard. They had very little money, and that first summer when Carlonna was pregnant was a scorcher. A friend invited Carlonna to a Mary Kay Cosmetics conference, and she came back and told Tom, "We've got to find a church." The Mary Kay motto is "God first; family second; career third." That made a lot of sense to both of them so they began attending a large church, believing that they could slip in and out of the pews without drawing attention. They learned otherwise.

"Week after week," Tom says, "I would sit there thinking that the message was just for me." At Christmas that year they went home to Indiana for a visit and attended church. When the pastor gave an altar call for those who wanted to receive Christ as Savior, this graduate student in chemistry went forward. When he returned to school, he began to meet regularly with John Hall, the pastor of the church in Virginia. John gave him books to read, and Tom began to understand in his head what he had assented to in his heart.

While many scientists have a problem with Christianity because they find it incompatible with their science, Tom didn't struggle with it. Today he quotes Tim Keller, the pastor of the church they attend in New York City. (Yes, the same Tim Keller that had such an impact on Katherine Leary.) Keller said that if you have a magnificent gift given to you, you don't ask the giver, "How did you make it?" You ask, "What's it for?" "I believe," Tom adds, that "because we live in a fallen world, we're not going to understand completely what God has created."

While in graduate school, Tom discovered his own gift of creativity in the field of biology. He worked with several professors and developed a product for oral rehydration—an antidote for the diarrhea that takes the lives of so many children in poor countries. Tom's creativity ran not only to new things but finding uses for them and getting them patented and sold to companies. All this led to Tom believing that he should go on to do some postdoctoral studies. They went to New York where at Columbia University he began to study under an internationally known professor of chemistry named Ronald Breslow. Breslow had begun a company called Aton Pharma for one anti-cancer product he had developed, and he asked Tom to come and run the company. Now Tom is the director of Discovery Chemistry for Aton Pharma, which produces anti-cancer drugs. "I really don't know how I come up with the ideas that I do. I'm good at it and that's all there is to it," he says, acknowledging that the gift has come from God.

Tom expresses his faith on the job by trying to be excellent in what he does. And at the same time, he and Carlonna are finding that living in New York City is a growing and learning experience. "You can't live in this city and be independent," he says. "This is a hard place to live, and you soon learn you need other people."

Who's in Charge?

Neither Katherine Leary nor Tom Miller would have planned their lives and careers exactly as they have worked out. But both would answer our original question, "Do I have a choice?" by pointing to a passage in the second chapter of Paul's letter to the Philippians, which reads, "Your attitude should be the same as that of Christ Jesus: Who, being in very nature God, did not consider equality with God something to be grasped, but made himself nothing, taking the very nature of a servant, being made in human likeness. And being found in appearance as a man, he humbled himself and became obedient to death—even death on a cross!" (2:5–8 NIV). This idea of being a servant and being humble cuts across the grain of this generation, which asserts its own autonomy and has lost respect for authority. We may understand how this popular attitude developed as we look at the mess that our national and international leaders have made of the world, but we err if we then substitute our finite wisdom and our own ideas and plans. Take a look at the wonder of your own body, then at the complexity of the physical world around you, and ask yourself if the one who created all this is capable of directing your life and finding the best place for you in his creation.

The biblical prophet Isaiah wrote, "Woe to the one who argues with his Maker—one clay pot among many. Does clay say to the one forming it: What are you making?" (Isa. 45:9). Can you imagine challenging the one who created you by insisting on your own plans? This topic of "calling" brings us to the great biblical truth that we live in a fallen world. While our abilities are limited, especially the ability to see the future, we desperately want to plan our own lives and have our own way. The desire to run our own little world, if not the world of others, goes deep. The Bible calls this sin. It amounts to trying to be God. "Now we see but a poor reflection as in a mirror" (1 Cor. 13:12 NIV). Someday we'll see it all and understand, but we now have a very limited understanding of the world. How can anyone of us in his right mind even want to try and map out our future when the God who created us, with all his omniscience and omnipotence, has already done it? And he will reveal it to us if we seek it.

Do you have any rights? Wrong question. Yes, you have the ability to map out your life if that's what you really want to do. The question is, who do you want to plan your life?

To Ask Yourself and Others

1. Have you ever messed up your life by trying to run it yourself instead of turning to God? Explain that!
2. Look at Philippians 2:5–8 and explain why this is such a great example of submission to God and of humility.
3. Do you think that if you planned out your own life it would be the same as what God has planned for you? Why or why not?

CHAPTER 9

The Childhood Dream

What do you want to be when you grow up?" How many times were you asked that question long before you had any idea in life what your options were? Perhaps you dreamt of being an astronaut or teacher or fireman or nurse or some other job that seemed glamorous. Most of us outgrow those kinds of aspirations, but some fixate early on a particular career choice and stick with it.

Bonnie Straka was one of those. As a small child she would creep into her grandfather's study and look at the pictures in the books on his shelf. Dr. George Lewis was a dermatologist, and Bonnie's grandmother didn't approve of her looking at those nasty pictures; she didn't think it was healthy for a little girl. (Skin lesions and rashes are not things of beauty.) Bonnie recalls that she found them fascinating.

Although her grandfather died when she was six, Bonnie remembers having tea with him, listening to him tell stories and telling him, "When I grow up, I'm going to be just like you." She also remembers her grandmother talking about him and how he'd help poor people who couldn't afford medical help. What she didn't know then was that he was a giant in the field of dermatology, one of the top dermatologists in the world.

From that point on, everything in her life became a step toward becoming a medical doctor. As a teenager she would lie in bed and dream not about boys but about winning a prize for curing cancer. She had no problem answering the question about what she wanted to do when she grew up although one well-meaning person once looked at her and asked, "Why don't you want to become a nurse?" That was not even an issue for Bonnie. She had no doubt that she could become a doctor if she wanted to, and that's what she wanted. And for years her mother had introduced her as, "This is my daughter, Bonnie. She's going to be a doctor."

She still had some tests along the way, however. At Williams College she met Andy Straka and they got engaged. This had not been part of her life plan, and she began to wonder how she could cope with her first year of medical school and her first year of marriage at the same time. Meanwhile, she was accepted in the premed program at Dartmouth. Wisely, but with fear and trembling, she went to the academic officials at Dartmouth and asked if she could defer her entrance for a year. It was an unusual request, but they granted it, so they went off to New York City where Andy got a job as a publisher's rep and Bonnie went to work as a marketing rep for IBM. Together they began paying off student loans.

After several years of this and of not going back to school, Andy asked her one day if she still wanted to go to med school. She said yes, and he said he felt she should, so she began the application process again and ended up going to the University of Connecticut.

While in med school she began to think about what specialty she'd like to work in and found that many attracted her—neonatal medicine, obstetrics, emergency medicine, trauma surgery, internal medicine. "I wanted to fix things. I'm good with my hands, and I learned that I have more of a surgeon's mentality than an internist's mentality. I like to make things better not only manage chronic problems." Finally she decided she wanted to do plastic surgery.

During her fourth year in med school, she got pregnant and delivered their first child just before she went to interview for the plastic surgery program at Yale. There she looked around and thought, *I don't fit here; they are mostly high-powered, single males.* People told her that if she was married, don't expect your marriage to last. Now she recalls, "I didn't dare tell them I had just had a baby. But I kept thinking, *Who will I be seven years from now? Will I have a marriage? Will I be rough and tough around the edges because that's what I have to do to survive?*"

At the eleventh hour before she had to make a commitment on a program choice, she was doing a dermatology rotation as part of the regular med-school program. One of the physicians asked her what she was planning to specialize in and she replied, "Plastic surgery."

"Really?" this doctor asked. So Bonnie explained her reasoning, and the doctor, replied, "Didn't you just have a baby? How are you going to do both? If I were in your shoes I'd do something else." The doctor was blunt; then asked Bonnie, "Have you ever thought of dermatology?"

So Bonnie did give it some thought. She realized that you can do a lot of surgery in dermatology, and she also had the visual memory necessary to remember recurring patterns, which is a necessity for a dermatologist. "I concluded that the Lord put this woman in my life to speak this truth to me," so, just days before having to make the decision, Bonnie inquired at Hartford Hospital to interview for a transitional program that was necessary before she could study dermatology. She finally went through the dermatology program at the University of Virginia Medical School.

For Bonnie the childhood dream has come true. More importantly, God used that childhood dream, as he often does, to guide her to the way of service for him for which he prepared her. Bonnie knows that she serves by being the best dermatologist she knows how to be and often sees the results of helping to "fix things." She doesn't think of her office as a spiritual "fishing pond." But God also gave her people skills and a love for the people he brings to her office. Bonnie often has a chance to reach more than skin deep.

One day she went to the hospital to do a biopsy, and as she walked into the room she felt the Lord was telling her to pray with the woman. She had never done that before with a patient and she kept thinking, *What if I offend her? What if someone walks in?* So she walked to the elevator and went down but couldn't escape the thought that God was bringing her to a new level in her relationship with him. So she went back up and into the room and with a shaky voice asked the woman if she could pray with her. The woman replied that that would be wonderful. And for Bonnie that was a beginning of a new dimension in serving the Lord as a physician.

In considering God's call, some people seem reluctant to ask themselves, "What is it I really like and want to do?" Unfortunately, some misguided souls think that if it's something *they* want to do it must be wrong. I knew a woman who, as a child, wanted to be a missionary to France. But she had this idea that God must have other plans and certainly not the ones she would think of. Interestingly, she married a man who felt called to the mission field, only she had the geography wrong. She ended up in South America.

Serving God through Architecture: Lori's Story

As a child Lori Snyder Garrett wanted to be a librarian. Her school librarian taught her how to file books, and she spent long hours in the comfort of the quiet library stacks.

Then one year as her family traveled across the country, she remembers somehow getting interested in mythology and thinking she might be a professor of mythology. By the time she was ten, however, she knew she wanted to be an architect. Her family had moved to Virginia, and her parents had bought a book of house plans. The plans fascinated the child, and on Saturday mornings she would spend her time drawing elaborate and inventive plans for houses. One house, for example had disappearing stairs, and another had a bedroom window from which she could jump into a swimming pool. Best of all, her parents encouraged her in this. Her family, who came from a Mennonite community, weren't wealthy, but they saved their money to travel, and when they did they visited museums and encouraged an interest in art.

Meanwhile, Lori does not ever remember not believing the gospel. Her parents were missionaries for a few years, so she heard the message often and was taught much from the Scriptures. But during her early adolescent years, she questioned much of what she had heard. "I think it was the whole teenage girl thing that got too much for me—cliques and so forth, friends turning against me. I said, 'God, either you've got to do something about this, or I'll stop believing.' Well, it didn't get any better, so for about a semester I stopped having my quiet time and I stopped praying."

However, because Lori had her driver's license, she was called on one night to take her younger sister and some of her friends to a Christian concert in Richmond. "I think it was something one of the performers said," she recalls. "I had a really intense spiritual experience and felt God's presence and his love in my life and knew that he was pleased with me the way I am. That really changed me. I stopped being so inwardly focused, stopped worrying about popularity, about not having a boyfriend. My priorities shifted."

After high school Lori went to Messiah College in Pennsylvania and double majored in art and math. Her dad was a math professor, and while growing up Lori remembers her dad staying up with her late at night to teach her mathematical concepts. And she always intended to combine math and art, even while pursuing her childhood dream. After graduation from Messiah she went to the University of Virginia to study architecture, then took a job with a firm in Charlottesville.

Today Lori practices her faith and architecture side by side as she designs homes, offices, public buildings, and so forth. She not only has the joy of creating and using her gifts, but she has an opportunity to serve people. "The reason I became an architect had nothing to do with people," Lori says. "It had more to do with art and math. Now, however, I find that a lot of my fulfillment comes in working with clients, working out their ideas and dreams. Even if my clients have entirely different tastes than mine, I still find satisfaction in seeing them enjoy the results."

Both Bonnie Straka and Lori Snyder Garrett learned that in seeking God's call on your life, it is not only OK to ask, "What is it I really want to do?" but it makes a lot of sense. For them it turned out that God had given them those desires, as well as the gifts to do what they wanted to do, and now they serve God doing just that.

God Can Use Your Childhood Dreams

There is an old story about a man who passed a young homeless girl on the street one day, and while he never gave much thought to her at the time, he did notice her. That night while eating dinner he noticed the luxury of the meal he was eating as well as the comfort of his home. After dinner he went to his study and found himself thinking of this young girl. "Why," he asked God, "do you allow such misery? Why don't you do something to help that girl and others like her?"

Then in the quiet the answer came, "I have done something," the Lord told him. "I created you!"

This story reminds me that God didn't put me here by accident. He has a purpose for me in being here, and I need to daily seek what that purpose is. Many years ago I learned that his primary purpose in creating me, as the Scriptures make clear, is for me to love him and enjoy him. As Augustine, one of the early church fathers, said so many years ago, "Lord, you have created us for yourself, and our hearts are restless until they find their rest in you." Once we learn that, we then want to discover how he wants that to work out in our lives. Ask yourself, "What specific ways does God have in mind for me to serve him and find my enjoyment and rest in him?" It makes no sense that he would call us to himself to serve him but not give us the gifts, abilities, and opportunities to do that.

It's true that some childhood dreams are just that—childhood dreams: becoming the president, finding a cure for cancer, stopping all wars, going to the moon. We grow out of these, recognizing them for what they are. But for many others, those dreams have led to fruitful ways of serving God and lives of deep satisfaction.

Many of the people whose stories we've told in these pages did not discover God's *vocation* (the word means "calling") until later in life, partly because they never heard God's primary call to them until later in life. However, Bonnie Straka and Lori Snyder Garrett are not exceptions. Their childhood dreams were not accidents.

On the other hand, following your childhood dream—or following any call—does not mean that you will work in that field for the rest of your life. Forty years ago when men and women entered a field of service they expected that, like marriage, it was a lifetime choice. And for many it was. (How many older adults do you know who have done the same thing all of their lives?) But today, cultural changes have brought about a situation where it is common, sometimes even necessary, for men and women to change not only their jobs but their career fields. Technology has made many jobs obsolete. And in an unstable world where radical changes might come tomorrow, we find it hard to look too far ahead. So we have programs and agencies that help people refocus their goals and retrain for new careers. Some experts claim that the average person today will make three to eleven lifetime career changes. It is not uncommon today to hear about people in their sixties and older getting a college degree for the first time. Seminaries now report they receive many applications from men who have had a successful career in business or engineering or some or other field. These men have not found fulfillment in their careers and want to work in the church.

However, God is still in the dream business and plants career desires in many while early in life. Often we go through a series of such childhood dreams before we recognize that this one is it. What is it you want to be someday? Don't be afraid to dream, even to dream big, while you wait to see if this dream is one that God has given you as a way to serve him.

To Ask Yourself and Others

1. Think about what you wanted to be when you were a child? Why do you think you wanted to do this?
2. What is it you can do well that brings you great satisfaction? Do you think there is any chance that this is a clue to God's call for you? Can you use this to serve him?
3. Talk to the adults you know, including your parents, and see if you can find one who pursued his or her childhood dream. Then get that story and share it with others.

CHAPTER 10

Without a Call

God gives and God takes away. We deal with many losses in life—loss of friends and family, loss of possessions, loss of health, loss of jobs. We learn to cope with loss and to grieve our losses. In our culture, we tend to find our identity in what we do. Work is an integral part of who we are. We identify people as Bob the CEO of an organization or Carol as a teacher or Benny as a builder. And because our work is so much a part of who we are, it's especially difficult for us to lose a job or not be able to find one. We don't want people to know we've been laid off or, worse, fired. Nor do we want folks to think there's something wrong with us that we can't find a job. That's embarrassing and the equivalent of failure. So, when people ask the unemployed what they do, they laughingly say, "I'm between jobs." We also hear about men, especially, who were the breadwinner all their lives. Then they retired early but without daily goals, without somewhere to go to in the morning and get involved, without a purpose, they quickly fell apart, got sick, and, perhaps, died early.

Unemployment among the fifteen-to-twenty-four-years age group is becoming more and more of a problem in our world. Kofi Annan, the UN Secretary General, wrote that, "Rising unemployment takes a heavy toll among young people who are particularly vulnerable to shocks in the labor market. Lay-offs, restructuring, and insufficient opportunities to enter the world of work condemn many to a life of economic hardship and despair. We have seen, all too often, the tragedy of young lives misspent in crime, drug abuse, civil conflict, and even terrorism."[1]

So it may be instructive to look at the lives of several people who lost their careers and the hope of doing almost any productive work because of a terminal illness and to see how they handled it. The loss of a job can be traumatic; the loss of a career may be a major life crisis. A career loss may be even more of a crisis if it comes through failing health because the person is dealing not only with the loss of self-esteem in not being able to work but with the sickness itself and possibly the threat of death.

What God Wants Us to Be: Jim's Story

Jim Nash remembers his childhood as scary. His father was a small loan operator, and Jim remembers hearing shots at night. He was a fat and nerdy kid, and his parents got a divorce when he was small. He spent a lot of time at his grandfather's farm; he loved it there, especially caring for the animals. After high school Jim's father planned that he would be the lawyer for the family business. But one day his dad said, "You don't really want to do this do you?" When Jim said no, his dad helped him to get a job on a ranch in Colorado. That furthered Jim's interest in farm animals, which was developed even more when, after college, he went to Cameroon with the Peace Corps to do a survey related to large farm animals. That, in turn, led to his going to veterinary school at Auburn and eventually to work as a large animal vet. At that point he had found his career choice. He was so enamored with large animals that one friend said he had an inordinate love of the cow.

As a teenager Jim had fallen into drinking and drugs and was seriously addicted. He had also rejected the conservative Christian faith of his father. In spite of that, he was able to carry on successfully in his field, during which time he went through several marriages. Jim knew that his life was messed up and that he needed help. Through church connections his father had heard of a highly regarded preacher in the town where Jim was living and urged Jim to talk to this man. So Jim made an appointment with Skip Ryan, and on his first visit told Skip, "Listen preacher, you need to know three things: One, I'm not here because I want to; I'm doing this as a favor to my father. Secondly, I believe in God. I thank him for sunrises and sunsets and the world around me, but I don't ask him for a —— thing. And finally, I sure don't believe in this Jesus fellow."

Skip wisely replied, "We don't have to talk about Jesus. Why don't you just tell me why you're hurting." At that, Jim burst into tears and cried for the first time in twenty years. At the end of the session, Skip asked Jim if he could pray for him, and he made time in his schedule to talk to Jim at least once a week for several months.

Jim began coming to church although he often went directly to a bar after church. But he began to meet a number of Christian men, and as he now puts it, "They loved me to Jesus." He especially remembers standing on the sidewalk outside of a restaurant one night after dinner with several men from the church. As they talked about their lives, one man began telling Jim that what's important to him was that he had a personal, daily relationship with Jesus. That stuck with Jim and became a turning point and a fixture of his Christian life. From then on he cultivated the practice of a daily quiet time to meet with the Lord. He also enrolled in an outpatient recovery program and began attending Alcoholics Anonymous.

Jim remained sober and clean over the years as he got involved in various ministries to the poor, including work in developing countries with groups such as World Vision and Christian Veterinary Missions. Then he married and settled down to a veterinary practice with large animals. Jim is a long, lanky, very friendly, and congenial man, and he found satisfaction not only in working with animals but more with becoming a friend to the farmers. "I especially love helping them solve their problems. Veterinary work requires using both your hands and your intellect."

Jim had just observed his fourteenth anniversary of sobriety when the hammer fell. He was diagnosed with lung cancer and had a lung removed. Anticipating going back to his practice, he became discouraged when it took him a long time to recover, and finally the doctors told him he would never be able to go back to his work. Working with large farm animals takes a lot of energy and strength, and they expected he would never have that again. The heaviest blow came months later when the doctors diagnosed metastasized melanoma, a particularly aggressive form of cancer and told him he had less than a year to live.

"I felt frightened," he said. "And I felt useless. I asked God what he could do with someone with only one lung. *What am I supposed to do?* I wondered. I felt I was going to be a burden on my wife, and I worried about our financial situation. I began to stay in bed longer in the morning and I fell into a deep depression." With the help of the doctors and his wife and regular prayer, he began to come out of that depression and to look at his life differently. At that point he began to pray, "Lord, if I have a limited time to live, I want to finish well." And he began to realize the primary truth that when God calls us he doesn't call us to do something; he calls us to be something. We are to be his child who he is forming in his image. And no matter what our health or strength, we can be what he wants us to be.

A Call to Comfort in Crisis: Beth's Story

Beth Fletcher Brokaw learned that as well. Beth has roots in Staunton, a town about midway in Virginia's Shenandoah Valley and once known as the Queen City on the Great Wagon Road. Over several hundred years, the wholesome climate and environment of the valley has bred some of the hardiest Americans and Beth fits easily on that list.

She was a good student and also deeply involved in service movements. Never one to sit still, she started a conservation club and became a cheerleader. "At the same time," she says, "I began my own secret pursuit of God, and at night I'd pull out a Bible and read." The valley where she lived is rich in the history of our country, but Beth was fascinated more with biblical times and lands and was a bit disappointed that she lived in twentieth-century America. It seemed so humdrum. Beth began to turn her life more toward others and less toward a pursuit of high school popularity, which was a big draw in her little town. She let go of cheerleading to have more time to help needy children in the community. She became the director of high school volunteers to encourage classmates to join her in the Big Brother/Big Sister program and in outreach to disabled and blind children.

And she kept trying to find this God she was reading about in the Bible. "I began visiting youth groups—Baptist, Methodist, all types—and my parents encouraged this. But I really couldn't find one that I experienced as spiritually alive." Then a friend who had been in and out of the "Jesus movement" in the early seventies took her to a meeting where she could witness firsthand this curious cultural movement. "As I listened and watched," she recalls, "I knew these people knew the Jesus I had been reading about in a way I hadn't experienced. I started talking to them and made a personal commitment to Christ. And that changed everything.

Before, I had been trying to find God desperately. Now I knew he had found me. He was with me, whether I was riding horseback at my grandfather's farm or whether I was working with needy children in my community. He was with me and calling me to reach out to others with the Spirit that was so profoundly filling my own heart. My calling to help the poor and needy now seemed empowered by a big God behind those childhood leanings."

Beth knew early on that she wanted to study psychology. She was thinking in terms of social work in which she would be doing hands-on kinds of tasks to help people in need. And while at Muhlenberg College she spent a semester in Harrisburg as an intern in a Mennonite counseling facility. When she graduated from Muhlenberg, she went to Columbia University in New York City, pursued a master's degree in social work, and then took a job back at the Mennonite psychiatric hospital in Pennsylvania. "I think this was one of the best facilities I ever worked in," Beth says. "They were using both psychology and spiritual principles in a very effective way." And this combination of understanding and helping people through psychology as well as through biblical principles became a driving force in Beth's life. "I look back now," she says, "and realize that I was only twenty-three years old. What did I know about anything? How could I help anyone?" Yet she did much family therapy with Amish and other rural families. They might never have shown their faces in a place like that except that it felt spiritually safer than other mental health clinics, and they so desperately needed help for depression and other disorders that were undoing their families.

In 1980, a significant relationship prompted Beth to move to California. Once there, she thought she would pursue a more specific dream she had for years—to work with emotionally distressed children. She became a social worker at a treatment center for children in Hollywood. In that process, she realized that while she enjoyed working with the children, she was drawn ever more to working with their parents and the other childcare workers working with the children. Trying out an old dream and a new challenge helped clarify more specifically where her interests and skills, and God's calling, rested for her.

A few years later, when she returned to her native Virginia, she tried another venture within the helping professions. She began offering crisis intervention at the emergency room of the University of Virginia Medical Center, where she could further expand her skills within the medical arena of needs. She also had the dream of pulling together churches and the mental health community, of tying together counseling principles and biblical principles. Soon she began helping a local church expand their counseling services and their training of church members in counseling skills. She realized this was her call—to offer counseling from a spiritually sensitive perspective and to train others in that mission as well. But she had a yearning to learn even more about integrating psychology and spirituality and to be as well trained as the psychologists she had worked with at the Mennonite hospital of her early training years.

Clear in her calling, she moved back to California where she took courses at Fuller Seminary and then entered a doctoral program at Rosemead School of Psychology. There she was able to further develop her abilities and understanding of how broken lives and relationships can be restored through healing therapy relationships based on both spiritual and psychological truths. In the process of becoming a clinical psychologist, she met another psychologist from Virginia, David Brokaw, fell in love, and married. Five days after their daughter, Laura, was born, Beth was diagnosed with breast cancer. She had begun teaching in the psychology program at Rosemead and had a counseling practice, working especially with people who wanted to wrestle not only with their own struggles within themselves and in their relationships but also in their relationship with God. She notes, "I often saw people who came from fundamentalist backgrounds who never experienced God as loving and never learned the joy of a relationship with him. I felt so drawn to this work. It was a very strange feeling to feel so called to this profession and then to be felled by cancer."

Beth received treatment and much prayer, took good care of herself, and the cancer went into remission. At the same time she discovered another calling—being a mother. Four years later the doctors could find no sign of cancer, so Beth and David adopted an infant they named Nathan. "I don't think you can find anything that brings a greater relational change in a person's life," Beth says emphatically, "than becoming a parent. That is now my call, and God couldn't give me a better one. My children train me as much as I train them, and my desperate plea now is that I'll be able to follow through on this call."

Beth was relishing this call as a mother and had also gone back to her practice when the doctors discovered the cancer had metastasized throughout her bones. She stopped teaching immediately and transferred most of her patients, but a handful wanted to stay with her. It's one thing to stop working as a baker or even as a lawyer or broker. But counseling is all about building relationships with people. In helping them work through earlier relational disappointments, the counselor is also offering them a new experience of safe and caring relationship, hopefully one which may even invite them to experience God as more loving as well. But what was this new twist in the counseling process teaching Beth or her clients? And how was it involving a loving God? It was not offering them a rosy safe healing experience. But it was teaching them to process hard truths and feelings about life and death and about God in the process. It was teaching them to hold on and to let go, to mourn and to hope, and to stay in relationship with others and with God through it all.

For Beth to walk with other hurting people while trying to deal with her own imminent death and, at the same time, be available for her family was the hardest work she had ever done. "I had trained all my life to work with people on difficult traumas and relational issues. But now I had to wade into this process in a deeper personal and professional way than ever before. It was agonizing at times, and yet there were also strange moments of joy and love—a taste of connection so deep that God was indeed smiling broadly in the process. God came down in some of those sessions and did a more powerful work than I had ever seen before." As she began to let go of this practice that she found so fulfilling, she became aware of how powerful a calling Christian counseling was, for herself and for many others. "What I've always wanted to do is help to change lives for God. I've had to grieve this loss, but it has made me an advocate for the field."

When she was diagnosed with metastasized breast cancer three years ago, one doctor told her that there was a 95 percent chance she'd be dead in two and a half years. She has had one round of chemo treatments after another; when one stops working, her oncologist tries something else. She has cancer throughout her bones and lives knowing that she could take a turn for the worse and die at anytime or live many more years. In the meantime, she has curiously lived more life than she thought possible in the midst of juggling motherhood and career. And in the many losses, of body parts and work and dreams, curiously God has offered her a deeper taste of his comfort than she ever "got" before. That experience of comfort has molded her heart for helping others, including her children, in new and different ways than her academic degrees or work experiences of earlier years did. Reflecting God in helping the needy sometimes has meant being honest with and about him in the midst of her own needs, a strange turn in her calling—but true to God's call nonetheless. In all her career moves, she never quite prepared for helping herself and others face dying, or living in the face of such deep loss, but that is what God is teaching her now. And curiously in her time left, that may just be God's main call for her.

God Wants Our Hearts

Few of us will have to deal with the grief of losing a career although many may have to deal with the grief of losing a job or the struggle to find one or the confusion of not knowing what God has in mind for us in the years to come. At sometime you may have to deal with the indignity and/or embarrassment of being unemployed, and at that point you may struggle with a sense of low self-esteem. Or you may be called to support someone facing the loss of a job or career.

Let's face it, our society reserves its honors for those who produce and for those who accomplish good works. But none of us are indispensable to the work of the kingdom. God is not impressed with our contributions to improve his world, and we need also to remember that nothing we can do can cause God to love us anymore than he does. He may give us success in the career to which he has called us, but what he really wants from us, as well as from the clerk at the deli counter and from the top men and women in government and business, is our hearts. Accomplishments, awards, and service records will fade away. Knowing God will last forever!

Many young people today have heard Christ's primary call to come to him and have a desire to follow and serve him. They are believers who are growing in the faith but have not been able to determine where and how God wants them to serve for the rest of their lives. That's OK. We don't need to have a life plan—or even a five-year plan—on how we'll serve God. If we're consistent in seeking his kingdom and his will, we may be certain that we are where he wants us to be right now, and that's where we're supposed to be serving him.

To Ask Yourself and Others

1. How do you think you could minister to someone who has lost a job and is having difficulty finding one? What would you say to him or her that is not patronizing but encouraging?
2. How important is it to your well-being to succeed? If you fail at something you believe is important, how will you handle that?
3. Do you think you are in danger of relying on your good performance in this world for your happiness?

Part 3

The Call to the Church

Throughout the two thousand years of Christianity it has been common to designate some vocations, activities, and places as "religious" and others "secular." This is a dualism that may result in repressive behavior or legalism or make it more difficult to hear God's voice.

For example, we call our church buildings "the house of God," and we often behave as though God actually lives there, so we require special reverence while in the building. In some churches it appears that more formal dress is required, as though God may not find our worship acceptable if we came in jeans and a T-shirt. Then little boys who race up and down the halls of the church building are told that they can't do that because this is God's house. However, the building in which we worship is simply concrete, wood, and glass. The believers are the true church, whether they are in the building or out of it. The Lord lives in his people not in a building. We are Christ's body, his visible church. I suspect that the Lord takes great delight in seeing children harmlessly enjoying themselves in the building where we worship and thereby acquiring a desire to return there as a place of joy. An extreme example of this is when someone seriously asks, as I have heard, "Is it OK if I drink coffee in the morning while I pray?" When we transpose the question we see how ludicrous it is: "Is it OK if I pray while I drink coffee?" Of course it is, if your heart is right. In Psalm 51:16–17 David wrote, "You do not want a sacrifice, or I would give it; You are not pleased with a burnt offering. The sacrifice pleasing to God is a broken spirit. God, You will not despise a broken and humbled heart." God wants our hearts. That's what counts in his eyes, not certain prescribed behavior that some have tagged "religious" or "nonreligious."

Over the centuries, however, we have applied this dual standard not only to behavior but to vocations, designating some as secular and some sacred. We have established a hierarchy of vocations, positioning the call to be a pastor or a missionary as a higher calling—more important and valuable, perhaps, in God's sight—than that of a conductor on a Amtrak train or the engineer who maintains our local water system. Of course God does call men and women to vocations within the church—preachers, teachers, overseas missionaries, musicians, writers, and more—and it is valid to ask if this calling is in any way different than that of those called to work in what we like to describe as "the marketplace." Does God call these folks in a different or special way? Is there something about a call to be a pastor that is different than a call to be a butcher?

These are important questions, and these next chapters seek to answer them in the same way we've answered the basic questions about calling and vocation and work—through the real-life stories of those called by God to these fields.

First, however, it may be well to consider the old story about the farmer in his field who noticed one day that the cloud formations spelled, "G.P.C." Convinced that meant "Go, Preach Christ," he went and told the elders of the church, "God is calling me to preach." So, to honor his enthusiasm, the elders asked him to fill the pulpit the following Sunday. Well, his sermon was long, rambling, and boring, so after the service they called him to a back room, and one old elder asked him, "Son, did you ever consider that, perhaps, G.P.C. means, 'Go, Plant Corn'?"

CHAPTER 11

A Unique Call

In an interview in *Leadership* magazine, a pastor named Erwin McManus talked about his call to serve God as a pastor. While in college as a new believer he said to his Christian friends, "It's going to be amazing when all of us, all over the world, are preaching the Scriptures!"

"What are you talking about?" his friends said. "We're not going to do that."

Well, that was the first time Erwin had any hint that "ministry" wasn't something every Christian did.

"Later," he said, "I visited the church where I came to faith in Christ, and I heard about being called to the ministry."

"What's this?" he asked, and they told him, "Some people are called to vocational ministry."

"I had no idea there was any distinction like that. So I went forward not because I felt any new calling but because when I came to faith in Christ I figured that's what you're doing here, following Christ. I didn't know you got paid or that another call was required to do ministry."[1]

I understand Erwin's confusion. Ministry *is* something that every Christian does. That's the point I've been tying to make as I've told these stories of men and women who know they are called to work not in the church but in what I've called the marketplace. The term *calling*, when limited to pastors, Bible teachers, and evangelists, implies that accountants, engineers, and life insurance salesmen are not called. I have tried to make it clear here that God equips each of us in some way to serve him and he has a place for us to serve.

I once heard about a thriving church whose members were reaching out to their families, neighbors, and their community. When these folks gathered on Sunday morning to worship, the common question they would ask one another was, "How is your ministry going?" The underlying assumption was that every believer was involved in some kind of ministry. Their ministry was not necessarily organized by the church, but they were ministering to someone or some group somehow.

McManus uses the term "the ministry" in a traditional sense of those God has called to work within the church as pastors or, perhaps, youth pastors or missionaries. So, for this chapter, I'll use the term in that traditional sense (using quotes around it to indicate that it's a special use of the term), and we'll look at this call to lead the church and serve God in that way.

You've also noticed, no doubt, that I have not used the phrase "full-time Christian service,"—so often applied to those who work in the church and to missionaries. I believe the term is misleading. The men and women whose stories I've told here are serving God full time. Brian Wispelwey and Bonnie Straka, both physicians, serve God by helping people care for their bodies. Doug Wallace serves God by helping people to be good stewards of the resources God has given them. Malcolm Hughes serves God by reminding us through his art that God is the great Creator and by giving us a shadow of the character of God. Whatever field God leads you into, he wants you to serve him full time in that field.

However, we've looked at many other vocations, so now we

need to look at the particular call to serve within the framework of the institutional church. And this raises questions such as, "Is there something special about this call?" Is the call to be a pastor, for example, a unique call? Is it a higher call? Does God call men to this work in a different way than he calls teachers or artists?

Rick Warren, well-known pastor of a large California church, had gone to Dallas when he was young to hear W. A. Criswell, whom many considered to be the most outstanding pastor in America at the time. "As I listened to this great man of God preach," wrote Warren later, "God spoke personally to me and made very clear that he was calling me to be a pastor." As Warren left the church and shook hands with Criswell, Criswell pulled him over, put his hands on Warren's head, and prayed, "Father, I pray that you'll give this young man a double portion of your Spirit. May the church he pastors grow to twice the size of this church. Bless him greatly, O Lord."[2] Warren walked away with tears in his eye, but he knew then without a doubt that he was called to be a church pastor.

It happened a little differently for Charles Haddon Spurgeon. When he was ten years old and visiting his grandfather's house, a family friend took the small boy on his knee and said to the family, "This child will preach the gospel, and he will preach it to the largest congregations of our time."[3] In time that prophecy came true.

The famous evangelist D. L. Moody was drawn into his work slowly after a beginning as a Sunday school teacher and having a growing desire to tell someone each day about Jesus.

A Call to Missions: Josiah's Story

Each pastor and missionary has a story. Josiah Bancroft's story, while unlike any other, has similarities to many. When Josiah was young, the only thing he ever wanted to be was a doctor. His father was a doctor and his grandfather a lawyer, but both had a strong sense of calling, and for as long as Josiah can remember they conducted Bible studies in their home.

Home Bible studies were not common in those days, and Josiah distinctly remembers an angry woman approaching his mother in church on Sunday and asking, "Why do you study the Bible in your home?" His mother answered, "Because we find it helpful," and the woman indignantly told her, "I don't study the Bible. I just believe it." However, the Bible was central to life in the Bancroft home, and Josiah heard and learned a lot about it as a child.

Josiah recalls that he always wanted to and expected to be a doctor like his father. However, with the ability God has given us to make decisions, we don't always take the expected path or even the right path. For several years while in high school Josiah attended a military school and found many of his friends deep into drugs and alcohol. So he began living a double life—going to church and playing the part of a Christian in front of his family and the world but secretly doing drugs. When he returned to Birmingham, Alabama, where his family lived, to finish high school, he continued that life.

On Friday, December 12, 1970, he went to a meeting of Christian young people at which a teacher named Howard Borland was supposed to speak. Instead, the man stood up and said to the group, "I had a message prepared for you, but I'm not going to give it." Then he pulled out a pamphlet called, "The Four Spiritual Laws," read it to the group, and sat down and said, "Whenever you want to leave, you may." Josiah knew that pamphlet well. It was published by a group called Campus Crusade, and his father was on the board of the local chapter. Josiah had read the pamphlet many times.

Oddly, it seemed, not one student left the room. They all sat quietly, lost in thought. Finally a girl stood up and confessed some sin, then sat down. Then someone else did the same thing, and on it went for about two hours. Josiah had taken the hallucinogen mescaline before he went to the meeting, but he sobered up quickly. God began to work in his heart, and he heard the old message of good news in a new way. As a Baptist Josiah had sat through a lot of altar calls, and he thought he could survive this. He didn't count on the Holy Spirit, however, and finally he stood up, confessed to his double life, and prayed that the Lord would forgive him and change him.

The next morning he took out his Bible to read, and instead of it being a duty, he found he was hungry for it and he understood it in a new way and just couldn't put it down. He also began to tell people what had happened to him, and he saw others drawn to Christ because of this. He stopped doing drugs overnight, and while his old friends pressured him a little, it just rolled off of him. That was clear evidence to him that God was doing something. Josiah began to have opportunities in the church to lead and to teach, to disciple others, and to do evangelism. On top of that he saw strong responses to his ministry, and he thoroughly enjoyed what he was doing. Still, while a student at Samford University in Birmingham, he continued as a chemistry major, believing that he would become a doctor. At the same time he began asking questions of God, "Is this the kind of work you want me to do?" He began reading books about calling and asking others about their call to ministry. He noted in these stories two kinds of experiences: (1) the kind of call Jesus gave to the disciples and (2) the kind of dramatic experience Paul had had on the road to Damascus. He kept looking for this kind of remarkable experience, but it never happened. So, finally, rather than pray, "Lord, are you calling me to serve in the church?" he prayed, "Lord, will you please call me to this ministry?"

Even today he can remember exactly where he was when it happened. He had just left the cafeteria at Samford and was walking across the campus, heading for the chemistry building. He was passing the library and the chapel was straight ahead. It was a beautiful clear day with a blue sky, and he was praying as he walked when he realized that God had answered his prayer and given him the desire of his heart. He went immediately to the registrar's office and changed his major from chemistry to English. After that he switched from Samford to Covenant College on Lookout Mountain near Chattanooga, Tennessee. There he chose a multiple major of Bible, English, and philosophy, and he began thinking of seminary.

Josiah had another experience that helped to affirm that he had made the right decision. He was present when the pastor of his home church in Birmingham recommended that another young man *not* go to seminary. When the young man left, Josiah asked the pastor, "What about me?" and the pastor told him, "You're fine. Go ahead to seminary."

His father's response was also affirming. He knew that his father was pleased that he had been pursuing medicine. Still, when he told his father he felt God was calling him to the ministry, his father supported him. So in the space of several years he had experiences that, while unique, were similar to those God has used to call many men and women to ministry in the church. First, God placed in his heart a desire to do it. Then God gave him gifts for ministry and pointed these out to him as he used them. Finally, he used several members of the body of Christ to affirm that this was right for him. Those three experiences are probably fundamental to all who are called to serve in the church—a desire for ministry, the gifts for ministry, and an affirmation by the church.

Josiah's story doesn't end here, however. He went on to the

seminary then to begin ministry as a pastor. While in seminary he picked up the idea that when you went out to be a pastor, you started a church. The idea that you would take over a church from someone else never crossed his mind. The seminary in Jackson, Mississippi, regularly received requests from neighboring churches for someone to fill the pulpit on a given Sunday, so in response to such a request he found himself one Mother's Day preaching to a small group of believers in Jonesville, Louisiana, a town of twenty-six hundred people and the biggest town in that part of the state. There were about fifteen people meeting in a home, and Josiah had a vision of what that group could become. The folks in the group wanted Josiah to come and be their pastor as they began a church. Both Josiah and his wife, Barbara, whom he had met in college, were convinced that they were called there. Four years later they left that church to begin a church in Mobile, Alabama.

Someplace along the way, Barbara told Josiah that she felt the Lord was calling her to overseas missions, the implication being that if God was calling her he must also be calling Josiah. She told Josiah she wanted to pray about it, and he told her, "That's fine! You pray about it, but I'm not going." So Barbara did pray about it, off and on over the years.

The church in Mobile had a missions conference every year, and one year, while a man named Jack Chinchin spoke, Josiah felt that he should really listen. Then several things happened that got his attention. When the speaker gave a call for those who wanted to give their lives to serve as missionaries, the Bancroft's thirteen-year-old daughter, Elizabeth, sitting in the same pew, pushed past him to go forward.

After that, Josiah began praying differently. Rather than ask God to show him if he was supposed to be a missionary overseas, he told the Lord he was going, and if this was not a good idea then the Lord would need to stop him. Later on when they put their house up for sale in what was then a very depressed housing market, someone bought the house within thirty-six hours.

While Josiah prayed that the Lord would shut the door if this was not what they were supposed to do, the Lord kept opening doors although at times along the way it seemed perhaps that the doors were not opening. For instance, when he told the members of his church that he was leaving to go to the mission field, they were not happy, and two of the church leaders sat down with him and told him he needed counseling. Later this reinforced Josiah's conviction that churches in America are unwilling to send their best people to the mission field, believing that they're needed at home. The other side of that proposition, of course, is that God calls only the second-rate people to the mission field.

A church group in Germany several centuries ago had an interesting twist on who should go. Believing that the Great Commission to "Go, therefore, and make disciples of all nations" (Matt. 28:19) applies to every believer but that some had to stay home to support those overseas, they established a lottery to see who would go. They put the names of all church members in a jar and drew out names, and those whose names they drew were sent out as missionaries. Can you imagine the uproar that would cause if your church tried that?

Over the years Josiah has advised many people who are exploring the possibility of going into missions or into any kind of ministry to think of it as walking down a long corridor. "When you come to a door," he says, "try the door knob and see if it will open. If it does, go through it and keep walking until you come to another door and do the same thing." For Josiah and Barbara, this process led to an invitation by World Harvest Mission to go to Ireland to help plant a church there. Eventually Josiah became the field director for the mission in Ireland, as well as the mission's director of overseas renewal.

What Is "the Ministry"?

In his book *Called to the Ministry,* Edmund Clowney wrote that while we are all called by God to serve, the call to pastoral ministry is distinct from other calls. First he makes it clear that among believers there is no hierarchy. Because all Christians share Christ's throne, one cannot be higher than another. No, instead, the minister is a servant, like his Master. He is there to minister to, not to be ministered unto. The Bible teaches the universal priesthood of all believers; that is, we all have access to the heavenly holy place in the name of Christ. It is true that some are granted greater responsibility, but they have no license to abuse that by lording it over other believers. Instead, the Scripture teaches to whom much is given much is required.

Also, just as we have different gifts, so we have different measures of authority. Paul was given authority to build up the church (1 Cor. 10), and the apostles were called to be witnesses of what they had seen and heard.

Then as we read in Ephesians 4:11–12, "And He personally gave some to be apostles, some prophets, some evangelists, some pastors and teachers, for the training of the saints in the work of ministry, to build up the body of Christ." God has singled out certain men and women to serve in these leadership positions where they have the great responsibility of preaching and teaching the Word of God and leading the flock.

Declaring the Word of God is certainly a great responsibility that not all of us have to the same degree. This authority to declare God's Word—which Clowney refers to as the "power of the keys,"[4] from Jesus' instruction to his disciples in Matthew 18:18—is a two-edged sword. On one side it cuts away any tendency of the preacher to credit himself with accomplishing any good from his preaching. The glory in all cases belongs to Christ. It is clearly the

Spirit of God in our hearts that effects the changes in our lives, not the skill or wisdom or ability of the preacher. On the other side "it cuts away all rebellion against Christ's true ministers. If the authority is Christ's, it must be respected,"[5] Clowney wrote.

While the gifts of the pastor don't differ much in kind from those given to other believers, they do differ in degree. "God does call workmen in the Word with deepened insights to perceive the outlines of sound words and with anointed lips to declare them,"[6] Clowney wrote. Just as Amy Sherman has been given greater gifts in mercy than many believers and Doug Wallace has been given a high degree of the gift of giving, along with the ability to understand the world of money, so my pastor has been given a high degree of insight into the Word of God and has been anointed by God to declare it. This, of course, is the work of the Holy Spirit, and it is our responsibility to recognize and honor the gifts given to such men. And while we see from this that the call "to ministry" in the church is not a higher calling, there is a greater responsibility placed on those called to this type of service.

Clowney argues in his book that this special responsibility of the man "in ministry" should make all those considering such a call to pause and think deeply. We don't call ourselves to "the ministry." If God has not called us, then woe is us if we dare to attempt to take the part. We know from experience that if a man who is not called enters this work, or goes into "the ministry" for the wrong reasons, he will find great disappointment. I can't imagine, for example, anyone being naïve enough in this world to want to be a pastor to make a lot of money, yet I'm sure some have been attracted to the prestige and, perhaps, the authority and respect often accorded preachers. One thing is certain: Anyone who goes into the work of being a pastor who is not truly called is in for some very hard times and will not last long. Behind and beneath the public appearances and seemingly outward glamour is more often a very difficult life. Church people are fallen people, and while many care for the pastor, churches are filled with people with their own ambitions, insensitivities, jealousies, and so on. Rarely does a pastor preach but that someone doesn't find fault with what he said or how he said it. People can be cruel, hard, demanding, and judgmental and they can resist the truth. They can also be very hard on the pastor's wife and children. The pastor who preaches against sin risks offending some people if not many. Churches often have factions, and the pastor will get caught in them somehow. Even the process by which men are called to a church holds large risks. After being tested, interviewed, and thoroughly scrutinized, the candidate stands the chance of rejection.

One pastor told me that his responsibility in one church was to visit the elderly. One segment of those were mature believers who had arrived at old age content. They were finishing well, and it was a pleasure for him to visit them. But another group, the grumpy group, were discontented, obsessed with their aches and pains, and fearful of dying, and they constantly complained to him. He found it a difficult duty to visit them.

The ministry is so much more than preaching, teaching, and calling on people in the hospital. In recognition of the trials of ministry, my pastor would often say to his staff and his elders when they came to some discouragement, "Welcome to the ministry!" The work of the pastor is generally hard and demanding, and parishioners sometimes strongly resist his authority. So the candidate for ministry must be absolutely convinced he is called and be able to lean on this conviction when the going gets rough.

A very few may even be called to be martyrs. Almost all will labor in obscurity although a very few—a Charles Spurgeon or a Billy Graham—may achieve great fame. On top of all this, many men and women "in ministry" today live in near penury. The man answering such a call, together with his wife, must be ready to work hard and work for less, and to work most often without human affirmation, knowing, however, that he will someday hear the words, "Well done, good and faithful servant."

To Ask Yourself and Others

1. From your observation, what do you think are the gifts needed for someone going into pastoral ministry?
2. What about missionary service in a foreign country? What gifts do you think are needed here?
3. What do you see as the obstacles a pastor or missionary will have to overcome on the job?

CHAPTER 12

The Call that Keeps on Calling

We've looked at men and women whom God has called to work in the "marketplace." We've just looked at one man who was called to "the ministry" as a pastor then as a missionary. Every life and every call, however, doesn't fit neatly into one category or the other. My life and my call from God to serve him fall right into the crack between those two broad categories, and because many others may fall there as well, I'm going to tell my own story as an example.

I never learned to study when I was young. I didn't like school and I didn't do well. (For one thing, I was a dreamer and found it hard to concentrate on school work.) My goal was to have a good time, and I did. So when I arrived at my senior year in high school and was forced to think about what I'd be doing the next year, I panicked. I had done well in one subject—English. I saw nothing I could do with that one area, however, so I explored vocational training as an electrician or a printer, and I considered the idea of joining the Coast Guard.

For several years I had been dating a young woman, and, because her father was a deacon in a local Baptist church, I began to attend their church. (It seemed prudent at the time.) So I met with the pastor of that church to talk about my future and see if he had any grand ideas to rescue me from my folly. When he asked me what I wanted to do, I remember telling him that I wanted to use my life in some way to help others. I was quite vague and general.

He suggested that I go and talk with the dean of admissions at Gordon College, a small school in the Back Bay area of Boston. I was living in a Boston suburb, so I made an appointment but didn't hold out much hope. For one thing my grades for several years were hardly passing. Also, I came from a relatively poor home, and my parents could barely afford to pay their rent, much less send me to college. Neither my older brother nor sister had gone to college, and they were good students, so who did I think I was?

To my great surprise I was accepted "on probation" although later the academic dean told me that everyone is on probation. If they didn't get good enough grades, they were out. Because the college was close enough for me to commute from home, I was able to scrape up enough money for tuition and books for the first semester and work on Saturdays to earn train fare and lunch money.

Something happened that fall that forever changed my life. I was attending that Baptist church and that same pastor preached one Sunday on Revelation 3:20, which says, "Listen! I stand at the door and knock. If anyone hears My voice and opens the door, I will come in to him and have dinner with him, and he with Me." (I understood this to be Jesus speaking, and it made an impression on me.) But a week later when I attended the meetings of a British evangelist in Mechanics Hall in Boston, he preached on the same verse, and it really got my attention. My family lived in an old, poorly insulated house on a hill, and that cold November night the wind crept through the cracks in my bedroom as I opened a Bible and found that verse. Knowing that God was trying to tell me something, I got on my knees beside my bed and prayed something like this: "Lord, I'm going to take you at your Word. Please come into my heart. I want to be yours and know that you are mine." I could not have told you at the time that was a conversion experience and the point at which I became a Christian, but I know now that from then on my life was changed.

At the end of that semester, with no money to pay for tuition for the second semester, I dropped out of college and went into the army, knowing that when I finished my term, I'd receive money from the GI Bill to help pay for college. Exactly two years later I was discharged and, with a few dollars in my jeans, went back to college, picking up where I had left off in the second semester of my freshman year.

Again, I was not a good student, never having learned good study habits, so I didn't get good grades. Nor did I have a clue what I wanted to do when I got out of college. I had never thought too far ahead in my life, nor had anyone ever told me that I should. Most of the young men I knew at that school were studying for "the ministry," which meant they would probably become pastors. But I knew that I was not cut out for that.

In my junior year I worked on the school newspaper and wrote a weekly column. I also ran in the student election for the position of editor for the next year and won. That next summer, between my junior and senior years, I took courses in journalism at Boston University, which whetted my appetite even more for entering the field. That next year I made another important discovery. Not only did I have a consuming passion to write, edit, and publish, but I had gifts for it. With that discovery, I began to believe I was called to "the ministry," but instead of working behind a pulpit, my ministry would be behind a keyboard through writing and publishing. With that in mind, after college graduation I went off to take graduate work in journalism.

Someplace in those years, I came across the verse in the Bible that many college students latch onto: "Delight yourself in the LORD and he will give you the desires of your heart" (Ps. 37:4 NIV). I knew that didn't mean if I delighted myself in the Lord, he would give me anything *I* wanted. But I took it to mean if I put God first in my life and sought what he wanted, then he would place in my heart the very desires he wanted me to have. Then I took the next logical step and believed that my desire to write and edit—the very enjoyment that I had in it—was something he gave me, and he gave it to me to use for him. When all that unraveled before my eyes, it was an awesome thought. And it still is an awesome thought today—that what I enjoy doing so very much is an enjoyment God has given me for his sake. My calling became clear. It is for this reason I believe that when we are seeking God's will for our lives, it is not only OK but makes a lot of sense to ask ourselves, "What would I really like to do?"

Pointed in a New Direction

I'm not sure now what started my thinking in the direction of missions, but my wife and I spent several weeks at a camp one summer exploring how I might use my gifts and training on the mission field. But because I was only beginning in the field and because I couldn't speak Spanish, much less write it, they advised me to get some experience on a publication and then, perhaps, later I could use that to teach others.

I finally took a job as an editorial assistant at *Moody* magazine, which was the publication of Moody Bible Institute. It was a good start. I had majored in magazine journalism, and magazines have always been my first love.

From this point in my life, I became very much aware of being called to what I was doing, which has always heightened the enjoyment of my work. From *Moody* magazine I became the editor of what is now called *Campus Life* magazine, and that led to the next call of God on my life. One day a missionary, the director of the Youth for Christ work in Lima, Peru, asked me to help him find a journalist who would come to Lima to train a young Peruvian man in magazine publishing. I knew many believers in journalism by that time, so I began to make inquiries, pass the word around, and pray that the Lord would send someone. Then one day I went home and said to my wife, "I can't pray anymore that the Lord would send someone to Peru to train this young man when there is no reason why I can't go." My wife agreed, as did the directors at Youth for Christ, so we raised our support and went off to Lima, Peru, as missionaries. After a year and a half, when I felt I had taught this young man everything I knew, I moved to Holland at the invitation of European Youth for Christ to do the same thing—help national youth groups establish magazines in their respective countries. In all this I was aware of God taking the gifts and desires he had given me and putting them to work for the advancement of his kingdom. In both Latin America and Europe, I also spent time writing about what God was doing in these places and reporting it to North American believers. I thought of myself as a missionary journalist, which was, I believed, the fulfillment of the call I had received many years before.

My odyssey of calling took several interesting twists and turns over the next ten to twenty years, including ten years on contract to a mission agency working in East Asia, for which I traveled extensively and wrote about their work.

In the summer of 2000, Mary and I went to Ireland with a team from our church to view the work of a mission agency. Mary has an Irish-Catholic heritage, and while visiting various churches there, she quickly built rapport with some of the Irish Christian women. It wasn't long before she began thinking about working there with this mission agency. It happened that Josiah Bancroft (see chap. 11) was the field leader, and after telling us they desperately needed help, he gave us the same advice he had given himself years before: Start walking in that direction, and if you come to a door, rattle the doorknob. If the door opens, go through it and keep on walking. We went home and did that, and a little less than three years later found ourselves living in the village of Bray on the Irish Sea about fifteen miles south of Dublin.

All the time I had been asking myself, "What is my part in the calling? Mary has just the right gifts for what this mission needs for its work among women. But I've spent a lifetime writing and editing and working in the publishing industry." I realized, however, that all my life I had gone where the Lord called me and my wife picked up and followed, believing that if the Lord was calling me he was calling her as well. Now I reasoned it was working the other way around. If the Lord was calling Mary, then he must be calling me too. After all, I can do what I do—write and edit—any place I can plug in a computer, and I believe the mission can find ways to use my skills and experience.

In our culture, where we tend to identify people with their work, it is a very strong temptation to make work the most important thing in our lives. I continually struggle with this. But, in the larger perspective of things, God doesn't need our work. He is more interested in *who* we are than *what* we do. *Being* must take precedence over *doing*. This is easy for me to write, but I confess it is not as easy to practice in the world that I live in.

To Ask Yourself and Others

1. Before you go any further trying to determine whether God is calling you into the marketplace or

into church-related ministry, have you answered God's primary call to turn your life over to him, to put your faith in him and become part of his family?

2. Do you think it's possible that God may be calling you to "the ministry"?
3. What is it you really like to do? Take some time to describe to yourself, then to others, what kinds of activities bring you pleasure. Do you like doing business, solving problems, creating works of art, teaching the Bible, building and doing things with your hands? Can you see in these something that may lead to a call for the future?

CHAPTER 13

So, Now What?

I wrote in the introduction that this is not a how-to-do-it book. We've offered no simple solution to hearing God's call for you because there is no simple, one-size-fits-all formula. Each life and each call is unique, just as the stories in this book have differed widely. There are no easy three or five or ten steps you can follow and be guaranteed to know exactly what God's plan is for your life.

Frankly I think it makes it more exciting, knowing that God has a plan just for you and that he is waiting to reveal it in his own way and in his own time. As we wait and listen, however—and that's a good posture to take for the rest of our lives—there are some guidelines that we can distill from what we've written here and from the experiences of the great body of believers who have gone before us. Again, these are guidelines, principles, to keep in mind as one whom God has given a primary call into his family and now waits to hear his secondary call to a place of service.

1. We Can Know God's Will for Us

This is a given that you can count on. God wants you to know his will for you. He has no desire or reason to hide it from you or to make it difficult for you to know. As you seek his kingdom and give him first place in your life, he will make his will known, using many means—the Scriptures, the Spirit, other believers, knowledge you acquire from other sources. If you have any doubt about this, read John 16:5–15 for assurance. This passage tells about the work of the Holy Spirit and how he guides us into all truth. Then read 1 John 5:14: "This is the confidence we have in approaching God: that if we ask anything according to his will, he hears us" (NIV). The overwhelming weight of the Scriptures tells us that God not only hears us when we seek to know his will, but that he will reveal it to us. The answer may not come the minute you pray. In fact you might have to wait awhile. God has plenty of time, while we always seem to be in a hurry. And the answer may not be exactly what we want to hear. But, make no mistake: He will reveal his will to us if we really want to know it.

2. Discovery of Vocation Should Be Made in Community

I believe our churches have not done a good job of teaching ecclesiology—which is the study of the church. This is complicated by the fact that our culture has glorified the self-made man. We idolized the frontiersman who went out on his own to make his way, and we make a big thing out of the do-it-yourself cult. Pop culture abhors dependence, and a popular idea insists that we can live our lives by ourselves, that each of us has the right to do what we want when we want to do it, as long as we don't hurt someone else.

This is unfortunate because the Bible teaches that all believers are part of the body of Christ and that we all affect one another. We don't live in private cubicles in this world, but especially, as part of the body of Christ, we are all joined. We are members of a local church, and we are instructed to submit to those who are placed over us. Paul wrote to the church at Corinth, "For as the body is one and has many parts, and all the parts of that body, though many, are one body—so also is Christ. For we were all baptized by one Spirit into one body—whether Jews or Greeks, whether slaves or free—and we were all made to drink of one Spirit" (1 Cor. 12:12–13). Then he goes on to explain that the ear and the hand and the foot and the eye all need one another. They don't operate independently. We have a lot to learn today about this unity and interdependency of members of the body of Christ.

Nevertheless, some believers go off by themselves to seek God's will, then announce to the world what it is they believe God wants them to do. When I was part of the missions committee in my church, people came to us and announced that God wanted them to go to China or Ethiopia or Brazil or some other remote spot to be a missionary. They made the decision all by themselves, never thinking to seek the counsel of elders or missions committee members or the pastor or anyone else. Of course they expected us to back their efforts and help support them. Sometimes we would have to say to them, "Well, God might have spoken to you, but he didn't say anything to us. And until he does, we can't support your efforts."

The affirmation of a call should be done in community. Seek the guidance of counselors, experienced people in the field of your choice, elders, wise friends, people who know you well.

You may need to listen to more than one person. We have friends who are missionaries in Ireland who fit extremely well into their position and are filling a need that not many people are willing to fill. Yet when they were preparing to go, they had family, friends, and business associates who tried to dissuade them and tell them they were needed at home. Some even told representatives of the mission that this young man was one of the best workers in the church. The mission representative concluded that this church was willing to send its not-so-talented people to the mission field, while it kept its best people for itself. That's where this couple needed the counsel and affirmation of other believers who could see through that fallacy and encourage this young couple when the doubts came.

The path to the goal is often strewn with obstacles—education, finances, poor health, interviews—all kinds of hurdles to overcome. And it helps to have wise counselors to encourage and pray for you when the going gets tough.

3. You Have to Listen to Hear a Call

Some years back when I was commuting from a Boston suburb to some classes in the city, I found myself trying to have my morning quiet time while I drove through traffic. I reasoned that I would be alone in the car with no one to interrupt me, and this would be a good use of my time. Then one day I came across Psalm 46:10, which says, "Be still, and know that I am God" (NIV). I began to realize that my reasoning and God's way of working were not the same, and that it was difficult to be still and hear what God wanted to say to me while I was doing 55 mph on a crowded four-lane highway.

I think this is typical of what happens to us in our culture. We run from work to recreation to home to shopping to meet friends to church and on and on. We fill our calendars, often even double-booking, and still we can't find time for all we want to do. It's the nature of the world in which we live. Then, in the midst of the busyness, we are assaulted with messages from radio and television, newspapers and magazines, billboards, junk mail, and so forth. Again, with all this, it takes real determination to find time to listen to God, to get away from the cacophony of the circus that surrounds us and truly be alone with God. But, unless we do, how will we ever expect the guidance that we want from him? A "call" presupposes that we can hear. It doesn't help if God is ready to point out to us what is best for our lives if we aren't listening.

So how does God speak? He speaks though his Word; he speaks through the Spirit as we take time to meditate. So often even our prayer time consists of reciting a list of things we want—bless so and so, heal the sick, provide for our needs—but we don't build in time to meditate on the Scriptures or only sit and enjoy God and listen to what the Spirit wants to tell us. Then, of course, he uses the body of believers to speak to us, personally or through spoken messages or through writings.

I mentioned in the last chapter that my wife Mary received the primary call to come to Ireland. Up until that time, I had answered my calls that brought me to various places in the world to serve. And because it seemed quite clear that God was calling me, it made sense that he was also calling my family. At the point he began speaking to Mary, I realized that he could use her to point me where he wanted me. We live in a Christian subculture where this rubs across the grain for many men, believing that they are the head of the house and, indeed, the Scripture teaches that. But the Scripture also teaches that we should love our wives and care for them in the same way that Christ loves the church (Eph. 5:25–28). Nothing in Scripture says that God doesn't call women nor that he can't use a wife as a means to pointing the husband to a place of service.

Whatever means he does choose, however, we have to be deliberate, especially in our overdrive culture, to allow the space and place where we may hear him, to allow enough margin in our schedule that we can relax and enjoy his presence, and find a quiet place where we can hear the voice of God.

4. Know Yourself!

Implicit in the proposition that God calls us to a specific type and place of service is the idea that he also prepares us. He gives us the personality, the temperament, the gifts and skills we'll need, and he opens the doors for the training and the preparation we need. If you're not good with details and don't have organizational skills, you can conclude that he won't call you to be an administrative assistant to a busy manager. And if you don't have a facility for numbers along with analytical skills, you're probably not cut out to work in computers or as an actuary or as a financial analyst.

The Dutch priest and teacher/writer Henri Nouwen had great compassion for the poor so he left a position at Yale University and went off to Peru and Bolivia to see how he could serve God there. He discovered, however, that he didn't have the gifts necessary for that work and realized his gifts for speaking, teaching, and writing could be better used on a university campus than in a developing country. He learned a lesson that many have learned—a need does not constitute a call. We can only be what God has made us, so self-discovery is critical in determining God's call for us. When he wrote his letter to the Christians in Rome, Paul emphasized this: "God has given each of us the ability to do certain things well" (Rom. 12:6 NLT). Paul described certain gifts and urged the believers there to note what gifts God had given them and use them (vv. 6–8).

Socrates is famous for arguing that we must know ourselves to be wise and that the unexamined life is not worth living. We need to know ourselves, the way God made us, as a guide to determining his call for our lives. We need to take a good inventory of our personality, our gifts, our training. We need to look at what we have done well and what we have enjoyed doing.

There are many resources available for this today. You might begin by taking the Meyers Briggs Personality test, which will tell you a lot about what you are suited for and not suited for. The test, which is available on the Internet, will tell you such things as how you process information, whether you are comfortable in an unstructured environment, whether you're an introvert or an extrovert, something about your creativity—or lack of it—and many other things to help you know yourself.

You can also find many psychologists in your community who are trained to interpret this test and to administer others that will help you understand yourself and your calling.

Begin by sitting down and taking your own inventory of yourself. Then talk to and listen to people who know you and truly have your good, not theirs, in mind.

5. Ask, "What Would I Really Like to Do?"

I believe that we can trust both our instincts and our desires when it comes to determining God's call on our lives. I believe that's how he works. We have to be honest with ourselves, of course. And we still have to listen to the Spirit as well as to voices outside ourselves. I have often looked at the success of several writers I know and, I'll admit, tasted a bit of envy. "Why haven't my books sold as many copies as theirs? Why am I not in great demand as a writer?" When I'm honest with myself, however, I realize that God has given them gifts I don't have, but that he has also consistently put me in places where he could use the gifts he has given me. So while I think I'd like to be a popular and famous writer, I know that's not what I'm called to be.

I wrote a little about this in chapters 11 and 12, but I'll repeat it here because I think it's so important. The psalmist wrote, "Delight yourself in the LORD and he will give you the desires of your heart" (Ps. 37:4 NIV). It may appear that the writer is saying, "If you find your delight in God, he will give you whatever you desire." I don't think it's quite that simple. I believe that if we find our delight in God, then he will place in our hearts the very desires he wants us to have. So, I believe, that my enjoyment of writing and preparing publications is an enjoyment that God has given me because I truly want to serve him and use the gifts he has given me to please him.

It has been clear to me since I was in secondary school that I don't have a scientific bone in my body. Science just doesn't interest me. Nor does engineering nor business. So that ruled out large numbers of vocations for me. The arts do interest me although I don't have the visual skills needed for some areas of the arts. Literature, history, politics, and social sciences have always fascinated me. So in this case I trusted both my instincts and what appeared to me to be common sense and stayed away from some areas and majored in others. However, I believe that all this was more than just common sense, more than my own reasoning, but the Spirit of God using my reasoning for his own purposes and guiding me to the specific places he wanted me to serve him.

6. Wait!

This may be the hardest guideline of all. We don't want to wait. Our culture doesn't encourage waiting to know anything. Information is cheap and easy to come by today. As I write, I hold tickets to fly from Dublin to Baltimore on Monday, three days from now, but today I read in the newspaper of a possible strike by the airport service personnel on Monday. I don't know if this will happen, nor do I know how my travel plans could be affected. Although I want to know the outcome now, I realize I will have to wait until Monday. Yet I hate waiting.

A few of the people I wrote about in this book have had indications early in life that they should pursue a certain vocational course. Most, however, could not and did not hear God's call until they were well into their training or even until they were well out of school. You'll probably have to do some waiting along the way, even if it's waiting to hear the results of a test or an interview.

This is where you'll need to trust God, to believe that he has your best interests in mind, that he has a plan for you, and that he will reveal it to you in his own time. And it's the very waiting process itself that God uses to develop our trust in him. For he is more interested in our growth in him and our preparation for life than in our preparation to do something. He is more interested in who we are than what we do. When I was in Sunday school I learned what my teacher used to call the Be-Attitudes, maxims that Jesus taught that focused on who we are. A paraphrase of the fourth beatitude reads, "O the bliss of the man who longs for total righteousness as a starving man longs for food, and as a perishing man longs for water, for that man will be truly satisfied." Waiting is not only a part of life; it is a part of God's plan and a means he uses to shape us more into his image.

7. Move Forward!

I know that I just finished talking about the need to wait, and now I tell you to go. It sounds contradictory at first glance but it's not. In seeking to determine God's call on our lives, there are many things we can do to move forward. It may mean taking another year or more in school to prepare. It may mean getting some kind of experience that you believe is not the final goal for you but will contribute toward preparing you for that goal. For Mary and me, trying to determine whether God was calling us to Ireland meant talking to scores of people, telling them about the need in Ireland and our desire to meet that need, then waiting for God to either provide the support we needed or shut the door by not providing that support. To learn that, however, meant we had to step out and do something, to make a lot of telephone calls, talk to groups, write letters, and so on. So we kept moving forward, and in his time God opened the last door and we arrived here.

Finally let's put an entirely different grid over this business of calling and say that every call needs to involve the following elements. And while these are somewhat repetitive, I think they are helpful grouped this way, which Josiah Bancroft suggested:

- **Willingness.** Our willingness to move into a certain area of work and service is a prime requisite.
- **Desire.** God often uses our own desires as a way to lead us.
- **Talent, ability, and gifting.** If God hasn't equipped us for a certain type of work and service, we have real reason to doubt that we're called into that field.
- **Counsel.** Guidance and affirmation from others—parents, teachers, church leaders, career and guidance counselors—all can help in confirming our call.
- **Opportunity.** Practically speaking, are you in a place to answer this call?
- **Internal witness.** Has the Holy Spirit given you a sense of calling and peace in moving in this direction?

To Ask Yourself and Others

1. What are the things in your world that could shut out the voice of God?
2. Who are the people or what are the communities you can look to for help in affirming God's call to you?
3. How do you feel about "waiting"? Are you impatient to know what God has planned for you? What do you think keeps you from waiting on God in peace, trusting him that he will reveal his will in his own time?

Notes

Chapter 1

1. Edmund P. Clowney, *Called to the Ministry* (Philipsburg, N. J.: Presbyterian and Reformed Publishing Co., 1964), 29.

2. Elton Trueblood, *The Incendiary Fellowship*, http://www.ivmdl.org/quotables.cfm?quoteid=226&cat=Calling.

3. Helen Shoemaker, *I Stand at the Door*, http://www.ivmdl.org/quotables.cfm?study=223.

4. Dorothy Sayers, *Creed of Chaos*, http://www.pechurchnet.co.za/resource/iccc2.htm.

5. Abraham Kuyper, *A Foundation for Trust*, http://www.meda.org/publications/marketplace/2001/mar-april-03.html.

6. Ron Hansen, *Writing as Sacrament*, http://www.imagejournal.org/back/005/hansen_essay.asp.

7. William Wilberforce, *Heroes of the Faith*, http://peterjblackburn.com/people/wilberforce.htm.

8. John Wesley, *Religion and Ethics*, http://www.bbc.co.uk/religion/religions/christianity/features/wilberforce/page6.shtml.

Chapter 3

1. Os Guinness, *The Call* (Nashville, Tenn.: Word Publishing, 1998), 29.

2. Ibid.

3. Ibid.

Chapter 4

1. Steve Stockman, *Walk On—the Spiritual Journey of U2* (Lake Mary, Fla.: Relevant Media Group, 2001), 100.

Part 2

1. Leith Anderson, "Called to What?", *Leadership* (Fall 2003), 26.

2. John Stott, *Complete Book of Everyday Christianity* (Downers Grove, Ill.: Intervarsity Press, 1997), 162.

Chapter 5

1. Helen Shoemaker, *I Stand at the Door: The Life of Sam Shoemaker* (Nashville, Tenn.: Word, 1967), 195.
2. Charles Spurgeon, *Spurgeon's Sermons* 4, http://www.ccel.org/ccel/spurgeon/sermons04.xlviii.html.

Chapter 6

1. Jacques Ellul, interview on vocation and ethics in the workplace, *Radix* magazine, vol. 22, no. 4, p. 12.
2. James Rouse, *The Other Side,* http://www.ivmdl.org/quotables.cfm?study=223.
3. Os Guinness, http://www.perpetuallearner.com/thecall.htm.
4. William Barclay, *The Letters to the Philippians, Colossians, and Thessalonians* (Philadelphia, Pa.:Westminster Press, 1975), 50.
5. John Donne, *Meditation* 17, http://www.imaginary.com/~borg/Literature/Poems/Meditation17.html.
6. Martin Luther King Jr., http://members.aol.com/klove01/marquote.htm
7. Jean-Pierre de Caussade, *The Sacrament of the Present Moment* (San Francisco: Harper, 1989), 63–64.
8. Os Guinness, *The Call,* 196.

Chapter 7

1. Jim Reapsome, *World Pulse* (November 8, 2002), 8.

Chapter 10

1. Kofi Annan, "The Global Crisis of Youth Unemployment," address on Youth Week, New York City (August 12, 2003).

Chapter 11

1. Erwin McManus, "Called to What?", *Leadership* (Fall 2003), 25.
2. Rick Warren, http://www.pastors.com/article.asp?ArtID=2718.
3. Charles Haddon Spurgeon quoting his grandfather, http://members.aol.com/pilgrimpub/calling.htm.
4. Edmund P. Clowney, *Called to the Ministry* (Philadelphia: Presbyterian and Reformed Publishing Co., 1964), 46.
5. Ibid., 49.
6. Ibid., 50.

TruthQuest™

www.TruthQuestBible.com

Get Deep. Get TruthQuest.

Am I The One?	0-8054-2573-X
Beyond the Game	0-8054-3042-3
Call Waiting	0-8054-3125-X
Plan de Acción (Survival Guide Spanish)	0-8054-3045-8
Getting Deep: Understand What You Believe about God and Why	0-8054-2554-3
Getting Deep in the Book of James	0-8054-2853-4
Getting Deep in the Book of Luke	0-8054-2852-6
Getting Deep in the Book of Revelation	0-8054-2854-2
Getting Deep in the Book of Romans	0-8054-2857-7
Impact	0-8054-2584-5
Living Loud	0-8054-2482-2
Something From Nothing	0-8054-2779-1
Strikezone	0-8054-3087-3
Survival Guide	0-8054-2485-7
You Are Not Your Own	0-8054-2591-8
Vision Moments	0-8054-2725-2
They All Can't Be Right	0-8054-3031-8
TruthQuest™ Devotional Journal	0-8054-3800-9
TruthQuest™ Prayer Journal	0-8054-3777-0
TruthQuest™ Share Jesus Without Fear New Testament (HCSB®)	1-58640-013-4

TruthQuest™ Inductive Student Bibles (NLT)

Paperback Bible	1-55819-848-2
Hardcover Bible	1-55819-855-5
Black Leather with Slide Tab	1-55819-843-1
Blue Leather with Slide Tab	1-55819-849-0
Paperback with Expedition Bible Case	1-55819-928-4
Expedition Bible Case Only	1-55819-929-2